Front-line Advent

Daily Thoughts, Prayers and Encouragement for Advent

To Jenny & Stephen
Steve Mor

Steve Morris and Barry Hingston

Foreword by Jonathan Aitken

Authentic

First published 2020 by Authentic Media Limited,
PO Box 6326, Bletchley, Milton Keynes, MK1 9GG.
authenticmedia.co.uk

Cover design by Arnel Gregorio of Arrow Designs
Arrowdesigns01@gmail.com

In the holiness of this brief moment
a bright soprano star sings in the sky;
the robin's song on the cradle is spent
in the holiness of this brief moment –
and the sleeping baby seems so content
with this winter carol, his lullaby.
In the holiness of this brief moment
a bright soprano star sings in the sky.

'Robin's Song', Denise Bennett[1]

Contents

CONTENTS

Foreword

This original, readable, and inspirational book deserves to become a 21st-century Advent classic. Compiled in the depths of the Covid-19 crisis, it speaks with both gritty pessimism and hopeful realism. The elegance of the authors' writing and the resonance of the new contemporary poems they have discovered reflects the dissonance of our paradoxical times.

Any buyer of *Front-line Advent* gets a literary and spiritual bargain. For this is a combined poetry book, prayer book, teaching book and a book designed to stimulate discussion by asking difficult questions.

Its authors, Steve Morris and Barry Hingston, are North London vicars from adjacent parishes. They are evidently men of wide human experience, sound biblical learning, wry senses of humour and original literary tastes. This makes a winning combination.

The poems which open each day's reading are remarkable. They challenge by their boldness and uplift by their beauty.

The themes of the book say much about the ups and downs of real life and little about the idyllic images in Advent calendars and carols. Yet, in these pages, the sacred keeps quietly pushing back the secular. The biblical passages are well chosen. The haunting poetry, the well-focused Scripture and the stimulation of the teaching all build a picture of mysterious anticipation.

Although the ancient paths of Advent are signposted, this is an outspokenly modern book. The traditional comfort and joy can be found, but its harbingers are of the new uncertainty and fear.

Earlier authors of Advent classics, such as Maria Boulding's *The Coming of God* and W. H. Vanstone's *The Stature of Waiting*, have soared through this Holy season on wings of prayerful anticipation.

Steve Morris and Barry Hingston are more down to earth but no less prayerful. They have connected the worries of today to the wonder of traditional Christmas. As the line in the last chapter of the book puts it, after praising the musical and artistic highlights of the season:

'It's just that Advent is also something else – the transformative impact of waiting.'

That hits the bullseye!

The Revd Jonathan Aitken
7 July 2020

Acknowledgements

We are indebted to the many people who helped us along the way in writing this book. Thank you, Patricia Oxley, for mobilizing a choir of poetic talent for us to use. We are grateful to all the poets who sent us their work. Jonathan Steffen deserves a special mention. Not only did he let us use many of his poems, he also wrote four new ones just for this book (Advent 1–4). We think that they are brilliant.

The Authentic Media team are an example of how to do book publishing. Thank you, folks. Thank you to Virginia Rounding who helped us with the manuscript.

Introduction

The Strangest Season

Steve Morris, The Vicarage, St Cuthbert's North Wembley, June 2020

Arrayed in circles, as in silent prayer,
The rooftops huddle round the Minster's base,
A congregation faithful in the face
Of all the ironies at which they stare.
This house of God has seen some godless deeds,
Deep desecrations wrought by faithful men:
The soldier's sword, the propagandist's pen
Have slain the Word they serve to serve their needs.
A single bell rings out, and out, and out,
As if each chime accounted one more soul –
A patient and persistent, untold toll
For every life the Minster lives without;
As if the timeless stones were God's own being,
Eternally revealed, with no-one seeing.

'York Minster', Jonathan Steffen[2]

We have, perhaps, all felt rather as poet Jonathan Steffen feels. It certainly might seem an odd place to start an Advent book. But Barry and I want to be real and for this book to be about all the ups and downs we face on the Christian journey. Advent is a time of darkness and light; a time when we get the very shortest day of the year. The birth of Christ is both joyous and perilous – it could always have gone wrong.

The poet looks at the amazing edifice of the minster and wonders about all of those who don't attend and don't seem to be alive with the love of God. He is struck by the indifference of people to the timeless God who isn't going anywhere. And he is struck by the harm done to the church and the faith by the zealous and the propagandists. Sometimes, I look out on my wonderful, but low-in-numbers congregation, and feel a bit like the poet. Where is everyone?

It is certainly true that right now the church is at a crossroads. Events in 2020 have asked deep questions of the church – how it is relevant and how it will change.

As we journey together through Advent, we can reflect on these burning issues and enquiries. We do it in fellowship and gentleness. We will be accompanied by poets and the writers of Scripture – who were often poets as well. Above all, we hope that this book helps us all to think, pray and be aware of God's presence. Plus, to live out again the ancient season of Advent.

The Advent Season

What are we to make of the strange unsettling season of Advent? At least it has always seemed a bit strange to me. Part of this is the time of year when it occurs in the northern hemisphere. The first day of Advent is when it becomes officially winter. During Advent is the winter equinox: the very shortest day of the year. It seems a very long haul before we can welcome spring. It is a time of thresholds: when autumn becomes winter and when the length of days begins to turn. Nature is expectant of change, and so are we. There is something just a little bit fearful about Advent. It is unsettling because it is a time of great paradox and mystery.

So, we are in the depths of winter and nothing seems cheerful. The trees and the grass and the flowers are in lockdown very much as we have been. Grey skies and miserable weather seem to reflect something of our inner state as well as our outer reality. Amid all the gloom, how might we begin to experience shards of hope?

It doesn't help that Advent has been widely commercialized over the decades. People associate Advent more with calendars than with the Christ. I don't altogether blame them. The problem lies in how difficult it is to explain the actuality of Advent. If Advent seems unnecessary, then perhaps we have only ourselves to blame.

Where I have wrestled with the purpose of Advent, is that this is a season of preparation for an event that we all know has already happened. That feels illogical to me. We *know* that Christ has been Incarnate among us. We *know* the story of Christmas; it's so familiar that it is difficult to live it anew, again. Some people just skip Advent and get to the Christmas party as soon as possible. Again, I don't blame them, I like Christmas very much as well.

The themes of Advent are powerful and, in some ways, primeval. Advent is about waiting – in hope and in trepidation. Chesterton said that the glory of the Christian story was that it was drawn in bold colours. If we get behind the grey, there is colour in Advent too. It is about the great battle between good and evil, dark and light. That battle is acted out in our lives and communities and in the heavens. It is when we think of Jesus' birth – the way he came among us. We also wonder about when he will come again – the first great event is always seen in the context that one day he will be back. It is also about our liberation from slavery, in the way the Jewish people were liberated too. Christ among us – as helpless babe, born to a poor family – is a sign that God is deeply involved in our world. It is his world, and he loves it and everything in it.

Advent as a journey

It might sound clichéd, but Advent is a journey. It is an interior and exterior journey. With the pandemic, we now live in a world where journeys feel much more dangerous than they used to. In this way we are probably a lot closer to those early Christians. We are aware of the perilous nature of life.

Advent is a yearly pilgrimage towards an event that changed the world forever. As we start the journey, the wise men have been on the road for months. They are ahead of us, but also full of expectation. As this haiku has it:

Ah, that star again.
I had other things to do,
But love does not wait.

'Christmas Haiku 2017', Jonathan Steffen[3]

Ah, that star again, we might echo as well. We lift our eyes again, from our own worries and internal voices and see that there is a star to guide us. We all have other things to do and that can keep us busy. The lead-up to Christmas has become deeply stressful as we worry about presents and decorations and the like. But Jonathan reminds us that, whatever else we have or had to do, there is something more important for us.

This book

This book aims to help us through some of the mysteries and delights of Advent but from a different perspective. Our aim is to give you something beautiful to read every day and something to think about and help you explore some of the underlying themes in this holy part of the year. We chose the medium of poetry because it seems to us that poetry speaks deep into the human soul. And we wanted to bring to you some poets you may not have heard of before. Each poem connects with some aspect of Advent, although many are not 'religious' poems.

So, the first part of every day's reflection is a poem, covering some of the broad themes of Advent. I have followed this with my own thoughts and a prayer. Barry has completed each chapter with some teaching based on daily Advent Bible readings and questions for contemplation. As the Advent season has a different number of days depending on how the calendar falls, we have included enough days to cover any year. If you are in a 'short' Advent, on 24 December do feel free to drop the extra days and go straight to 'Christmas Eve'.

Advent is a time of reflection. It is a time when we can have a mini spiritual MOT, not the full monty of Lent. We take a look at ourselves and all that is right and that which is wrong. We don't do this in a spirit of misery or self-condemnation, but in a spirit of hope that in the end all shall be well.

We wonder about the great theme of darkness and light. In some odd way we need to understand the darkness in order to appreciate the joys of light. We think about what it is to have faith and to be peaceful and to feel joyous, even when the world seems a dangerous and unreliable place. And finally, we look again, and try to experience again, the extraordinary claim that the God who made the heavens one day came among us as one of us.

To us, the Incarnation is something that fuels our ministries as parish priests. If Jesus was one of us and among us, then he has baptized the whole of life with his holiness. There is no such thing as an ordinary life or an ordinary person. If we accept this, then we go about life with more wonderment than we thought possible.

This book is our way of looking at Advent from the front line. We hope that it is challenging and thought-provoking. The teaching sections aim to help all of us to explore doubts, certainties and questions.

We are both ministers in parishes in north London and it is a joy. This book shares some of our joys and our frustrations along the way and we hope it will help you to appreciate again the wonders of Advent in the same way that writing it has helped us too.

I remind myself, just before we begin, of the big show that we are awaiting.

> Lovely boy, again it is your first coming
> and I make notes, guests, lists, the tree
> while you in that calm womb of hers
> wait patiently to be set free.
>
> You know already that your time is short
> for all your works of love, gnarled limbs made straight
> blind eyes unsealed and the nine lepers leaping
> on, on along the road and out of sight.
>
> I want to be the tenth who gave you thanks,
> who clasped your feet, looked in your fabulous face,
> thanking you now for all that is to come,
> your works of love, the cross, your work of grace.

'First Coming', Ann Pilling[4]

WEEK 1

Hope and Faith
(and Waiting)

The rot of autumn fills my breath and bones:
The long leftover leaves of lives I've left,
Downtrodden, cold and damp and dark, bereft
Of their own selves, anonymous as stones.
I walk a path that is no path at all
Through trees as dead as my own dangling hands,
Across these all-too well known nowhere lands
Towards a distant sky of darkening pall.
A robin would bring hope. A thrush. A mouse.
Some tiny creature just as lost as me,
Oblivious to its stumbling destiny.
A beetle, or a centipede. A louse.
Imagine that right now my footsteps trod
Upon the only thing that's left of God.

'Advent 1', Jonathan Steffen[5]

I think we might all be a lot happier if we admitted how messed-up we really are. The ghosts of all that we have been and done haunt us. But accepting that our lives are and have been messy is a great liberation from perfectionism.

The poet is wondering about hope. We've all wondered about that. Advent is the great season of hope, but hope is hard-won. It comes at a cost. In the poem, the skies are becoming dark and ominous. Everything seems dead and used up – the trees, the poet's own body. I tend to get very low by the time December comes. I miss the sunlight and the warmth. The poet wonders if a thrush or a mouse might cheer him up a bit. But then he gets one of those subversive thoughts – what if he treads on a louse and that is all there is to remind us of God's presence? That's funny.

So, this is where we all start Advent from. We are at the dead-end of the year and often feel at a dead-end ourselves. We bring to Advent all our dead-ends and begin the journey wanting to find hope – the big hope that God is with us and that we are right with him.

Advent Sunday

Is God Asleep?

. . . Why do you sleep?
    Rouse yourself! Do not reject us for ever.
Why do you hide your face
    and forget our misery and oppression?

We are brought down to the dust;
    our bodies cling to the ground.
Rise up and help us;
    rescue us because of your unfailing love.

Psalm 44:23–26

In some ways, Advent is a response to the cry, 'Where the heck are you, God?' Behind this cry is another one – 'We need rescuing.' I am sure it is something we have all thought. I remember once, when my family was having a particularly hard time, that I said the very same thing. I was driving home and feeling worn down and worried about how things seemed to be going. I remember shouting at the top of my voice: 'Come on, God, step up, help us out!' – well, that's the polite version.

I felt a bit better for it, and I am glad to report that things did start to improve. Perhaps my anguished question helped; I hope so. I certainly think I am way too polite and cautious in my prayers and dealings with God – treating him like an infirm aged relative, rather than the God who made the universe and, in Advent, was about to dramatically enter into history.

The beautiful psalm seems to have the measure of things. The poet begins by accusing God of being asleep on the job. He wonders why God isn't stepping in to do something about oppression and misery. It is a question that is as pertinent now as it was then. I, for instance, have no idea why God didn't stop the holocaust in its tracks, or deal with Robert Mugabe earlier or any other number of ghastly things and people. The forces of evil are all too evident, and of course that evil isn't just about other people and situations. We carry it around with us too – pride, selfishness, greed and the like.

That this psalm is set for the first Sunday of Advent is telling. The Jewish people were under the yoke of Roman oppression. Spies were everywhere, they were being bled dry with taxes and this proud nation was under enemy occupation. This is the ground from which the Incarnation begins.

Jesus was born in a particular time and place – both inauspicious. With the birth of the infant Christ no one could accuse

God of needing to be woken up from a deep sleep. He became an actor in the great story.

Recently, I was reading the Book of Job. It gave me more questions than answers. I find it a very hard read. What is obvious to me from this ancient Scripture is just how 'other' God is. God's justification of himself is full of all the mighty things he has done. But when I read it, I find myself not feeling very close to God at all. We are just too different, and he has all the power and majesty and I don't. But, as we go through Advent we see the other side, and we begin to realize that our God took the ultimate risk, not just to identify with us, but to be us – in all our contingency and vulnerability.

———————————

Prayer

Father, we begin this Advent journey with the year nearly behind us. Like all years it has been full of struggle and hope, joy and sadness. At times we wonder where you are and why you have not acted. Or perhaps you have acted, and we just haven't noticed. We know that your timing is perfect but here, bound by the laws of time and space, and afflicted with the ravages of sin, we sometimes cannot see your plans working out for the good.

Forgive us our impatience, but when we call to you and wonder whether you are sleeping it isn't because we don't believe in you, it is because we do. We know that your ways can sometimes be mysterious, but we are simple creatures and we cry out for healing, safety and hope. Lord, please be patient with us and help us to be patient towards ourselves.

Amen.

Teaching

> *Isaiah 64:1*
> Oh, that you would burst from the heavens and come down! How the mountains would quake in your presence! (NLT).

> *Mark 13:24–37*
> The sun will be darkened, the moon will give no light, the stars will fall from the sky, and the powers in the heavens will be shaken (vv. 24–25, NLT).

Advent Sunday – we start to look forward to the time when God bursts from the heavens and comes down, mountains quake, and stars start to fall from the sky. These are baffling words. Isaiah is speaking into the mystery of God's apparent absence, but insisting that he is always working, even when we cannot see him. Isaiah is giving voice to the common experience of God's apparent absence, by highlighting the fact that he is working as we wait.

So how is he working? As we commence Advent and journey to Christmas Day, we will encounter a lot of powerful imagery and language. The challenge for us is to not get too religious about it, consign it to the 'Tolkien' section of our faith. It's a good read, but not real. Isaiah and Mark meant something when they recorded these words, and if we do not take it seriously, we kick it down the road like a tin can. God is never asleep, he is invisible but never absent.

The hope of Advent is that Christ among us ushers in the start of a new world order. It is not something endlessly postponed but a hope we can work towards now. That hope is tangible and real, and God is working on it now, even if that is not apparent to us.

Of course, the stars cannot fall from the sky because the stars are not in the sky. The reality of this language is that it speaks to something much more imminent and possible, which is more exciting, not less.

If we project these events into the end-times, we rob them of their power right now. We feel it's OK not to participate in them, because for us they never happen. Advent opens our minds to the possibility that the invisible God is at work even when we cannot see it, and that earthly powers will crumble. If we just say that it will 'all be all right in the end', then we do not participate with God in resisting evil now. Those false deities are with us today – the sun, the moon, the stars, the mountains are money, sex and power, to name but a few. They are pernicious and infectious structures, affecting not just the 'sinful naughty world' but the minds and hearts of the church as well – we have our false gods. Both Isaiah and Jesus say, these will not stand because they are not of God.

Advent calls Christians to ally themselves to this earthly statement of heavenly intent. Isaiah calls God to come down, not stay in the heavens. The promise is that seemingly invincible earthly institutions will shake and fall because they are false. That is a hugely inspirational thing, provided we don't turn it into make-believe astronomy or endlessly procrastinated future hope, a tin can constantly kicked down the road into the never-ending future.

God is bursting forth from the heavens in Christ. The body of Christ (the church) is asked to participate in the ending of false deities and the construction of a better world. Each prayer, each Christlike act of kindness, is an extension of the kingdom of God, and one more false god on the bonfire.

'The great god Pan is dead' said Plutarch in the first century . . . the Incarnation is great news of hope. If 2020 has taught us anything, it is that the old gods have always let us down. God is anything but asleep. Advent boldly declares that God is wide-awake and actively engaging in history.

Questions

- Think about false gods – are there any in your life?
- What structures and powers would you love to see dismantled in the world?
- Do you sometimes feel God is absent, or even asleep?

Monday 1

The Business of Hope

These things I remember
   as I pour out my soul:
how I used to go to the house of God
   under the protection of the Mighty One
with shouts of joy and praise
   among the festive throng.

Why, my soul, are you downcast?
   Why so disturbed within me?
Put your hope in God,
   for I will yet praise him,
   my Saviour and my God.

My soul is downcast within me;
   therefore I will remember you
from the land of the Jordan,
   the heights of Hermon – from Mount Mizar.

Psalm 42:4–6

It is a question I have often asked myself: 'Why, my soul, are you downcast?' The poet seems to be feeling down because he is remembering times when he was happy, and they seem a long time ago. Most of us felt that way during lockdown. The old simple pleasures were taken away. We couldn't even go to church – which seemed particularly cruel.

Sometimes we look back on times when we felt very close to God and mourn that a gap seems to have opened up between us and him. It can feel something like grief.

Advent is about hope and faith. But hope's near siblings are darkness and fear. The Advent journey includes all of these because it is a time to be open about where we are and how we feel.

We approach the joyous day of Christmas but first we have to go through valleys and difficulties. I suppose no pilgrimage worth its salt is straightforward. There are times when we feel like giving up. The going looks too hard. Seeing these Advent weeks as a pilgrimage is helpful. Like all pilgrimages it does not do to do it alone.

In this week we hear the 'shouts of joy' that the poet mentions, only faintly. We hear them from the other room, from the distant mountain. But they are there and just because we might be downcast that doesn't mean that we won't experience them again. Of course, all the poet's hope is in God. The whole lot.

_____

Prayer

Father, we thank you for the honesty of the psalmist. We thank you that we can be honest when we come to you and not pretend that we are feeling well and happy when we aren't. It is a great comfort that Jesus experienced sadness and knew what it was to feel desolate. And so, we come to you in all our desolation but also in all our hope that you are the God who saves us.

In our communities, loneliness and desperation are every-where. People have been isolated and felt full of terror and uncertainty. We put that before you. We cannot explain it, it just is, and it is part of our journey through life. But our prayer today is that you will transform our desolation and help it to be just a small way-post on our journey. We pray for all of those who feel desperate today and we ask that they will be surrounded by friendship and help and that they would see the shards of hope all around them.

Amen.

Teaching

Psalm 19:1
The heavens declare the glory of God; the skies pro-claim the work of his hands.

Isaiah 52:7
How beautiful on the mountains are the feet of those who bring good news, who proclaim peace, who bring good tidings, who proclaim salvation, who say to Zion, 'Your God reigns!'

Matthew 4:18–22
'Come, follow me,' Jesus said, 'and I will send you out to fish for people' (v. 19).

The great challenge of my life has always been to link the great statements of the Scriptures with my real life. If it looks like something too grand and far reaching, then I find myself observing from afar, contemplating rather than participating. If it is too unreal, or too distant, or even too grand to relate to, then my downcast soul finds no material comfort in it. I lose hope rather than gain it. It feels like fiction, and it feels escapist.

I suppose what Advent really means here is God stating, 'I am coming to be part of you, so you can be part of me.' And that means that even when I feel lost and confused, he is still participating in my life. It cannot be meaningful if it is just escapism and pretend.

Read these Scriptures in the sequence Psalm–Old Testament–New Testament. It becomes a journey, from too-grand-by-half vastness to deep and abiding personal hope. It's a mystery tour of God's rule, from the testimony of the cosmos in Psalm 19, to one redeemed nation restored from Babylon in Isaiah, down to the intimate intention of God towards the individual in the gospel. We actually participate in this as 'fishers of men'; we travel a huge mental journey, from galaxies to our next-door neighbour.

God's intention is redemption – the restoration of all things. God is taking his cherished reality, his 'very good' created order, with all its shortcomings and rescuing it from chaos. No matter how bad it looks now, Advent is hope. Advent is the anticipation that God is arriving soon at the most intimate level, becoming a human being. His purpose is to redeem everything, including every human being. He will redeem our suffering and our hopelessness, and that is the substance of human hope. That glory persists even if we fear our best days, our best connections, with God are behind us, as the psalmist seems to believe.

God dwells in our reality. Part of that reality is sometimes feeling downcast and wondering where it all went wrong. Things used to be good, but not now. That is a reality for many. Isaiah gives us hope in a chorus of beauty in a dawning hope of restoration. The redemption of Israel from Babylon is not a one off, it is a pattern, and the calling of the disciples is the same calling we all have, to participate in this never-ending, intimate work of God.

If we just meditate on the infinite, we end up feeling insignificant and valueless. Peter Cook (1937–95) said it brilliantly: 'As I looked out into the night sky, across all those infinite stars, it made me realize how insignificant they are.' Many a true word. The coming of Jesus substantiates hope because he shows us that we matter to God (Matt. 6:26).

Questions

- Do you take any inspiration from creation and the universe? Can you see it as God's calling card?
- Similarly, can you relate to the same God who understands you, to the very number of hairs on your head?

Tuesday 1

Hope and Faith in the Wreckage

Amidst the hierarchies of dereliction –
The crumbling faces and the fading names –
It smiles in disconnected benediction,
Its hand raised to the sky from which it came.
How distant is that sky, how uninvolved,
How coolly grey and drab and blank and bleak;
How prospectless a place in which to seek
A sign that life's enigmas might be solved.
Does God exist? Did Jesus raise the dead?
What hand can smooth away our human pain?
The questions, like the angel's smile, remain:
A testimony to the word unsaid.
– Perhaps the gardener there understands,
A trace of heaven on his unwashed hands.

'Cemetery Angel', Jonathan Steffen[6]

I'm not sure many of us would go looking for hope in a graveyard. I tend to avoid them, if I can, because they make me feel unhappy. When I was studying for ordination, we did an activity where we asked people to name their great-grandparents. It was fascinating because almost none of us knew their names; and that was just a few generations ago. Their life stories had turned to dust and we were just vaguely aware that they had once been and once been something and someone.

The poet is having a bleak time of it in the cemetery. Confronted with mortality and dereliction he begins to wonder if this is the place where the great questions of life can be answered at all. Does God exist? Did Jesus really raise the dead? And, of course, there is that unanswerable question about the nature and actuality of pain. Pain tests hope as much as our faith. Of course, that's something that Jesus understood all too well as he cried out on the cross, wondering if his father had forsaken him.

All is not lost. It never is. The poet suddenly sees a statue of an angel. He catches its smile. He can't quite get rid of the questions, but nor can any of us. Maybe the angel's enigmatic smile is a clue to the wild hope that things might turn out for the best.

The poet wonders if it is the cemetery gardener who might know the answer to our great questions. After all, our Lord was mistaken for one. Perhaps this earthly gardener has a trace of heaven on his unwashed hands, perhaps we all do. In one sense we all have unwashed hands, but our brokenness in the end is no barrier to God. Of course, we can find hope and faith in the strangest places; even abandoned and desolate ones. Even with grubby souls we can take stock and say sorry to God and turn over a new leaf in confidence and faith.

––––––––––––––

Prayer

Father, in some sense we are just like the gardener in this poem. We stand before you with dirty hands, but we know that you see in us what you see in your dear son. We are grateful for that.

The image that the poet chooses of the cemetery is a particularly resonant one for us at the moment. Father, we have lost loved ones and friends and we mourn them. We weren't expecting this great pandemic disaster and change, and we look back and would like to have our old lives back. Perhaps we appreciate more what we had, now that we don't have it.

Jesus, you were mistaken for the humble gardener. Today we offer our prayers to you in that spirit; the son of God who walked beside us had an ordinary and everyday life, and will never let us go.

Amen.

––––––––––––––

Teaching

Isaiah 11:10
Psalm 72:1–4

Luke 10:21–24
I praise you, Father, Lord of heaven and earth, because you have hidden these things from the wise and the learned, and revealed them to little children (v. 21).

Insofar as my Christian life has been a struggle, it has been a battle for the mind. I am much more comfortable with intellect, but I am driven and fed emotionally. I like to explain things, rather than hug them and enjoy them, but it can leave me a bit empty, and sometimes sad. It also leaves more things unexplained than it explains, and that erodes my sense of trust. I'm a little like the poet in the graveyard – too many questions. Sometimes I need to become a child again and just enjoy the story.

Jesus' words today confront us with an uncomfortable truth which is at the same time liberating. God's redemption is harder to see the more you trust pure intellect to explain it. It is so easy to fail to see the wood for the trees that we need to become like children to see it again.

Comprehending it is something akin to being childlike. The childlike response is trust, just accepting the truth of something for now, until better understanding is available. This is different to the childish response, which says 'Tell me the answer – now!'

The poet above has just such a moment of trust – dim and faltering though it is. The smile of the angel simply says, trust. He is searching for something that feels hidden, and which may never be fully revealed. Faith, another word for trust, is the evidence of things not seen (Heb. 11:1).

The Bible's picture of this is too big and too mysterious to reduce to intellectual definitions. It is much better being childlike, glorying in the storybook imagery of hope as God lays out his intention.

Isaiah once again paints a picture, rather than giving a factual explanation, and it certainly begs a lot of questions! The future hope looks like a wolf living in harmony with the lamb, and the cattle with the lions. I can't relate to this as literal vegetarianism, but I can get very connected with the idea of the strong and the weak living in harmony, an end to predatory behaviour where no one is somebody else's resource to exploit. I can get excited by a world where the so-called 'weak' can flourish and express themselves. I can, like a child, trust in the assurance of justice, where the poor are treated fairly, and the land yields prosperity for all under the reign of a just king.

A childlike acceptance of that as a vision of truth engenders hope and trust without requiring an answer. I do not need to know how it will happen, just that it will happen. We do not need to kiss our brains goodbye, but just understand that all our theories are inadequate. The world will be in harmony with itself and if I align myself with making that happen, then I am doing the will of God. That sense of harmony, of things making sense, is what the poet is searching for on his lonely pilgrimage to the graveyard.

The wolf lying down with the lamb sounds like a great answer, I just can't know what the question is right now. I can find some hope in that.

Questions

- How do uncertainty and trust relate to each other?
- Is there room in your life for a bit more childlike faith?
- How do you interpret the 'wolf lying down with the lamb'?

Wednesday 1

Hope and Faith in Our Non-faith Times

It is a quiet deep evening outside
growing indistinct as blackwool clouds
sponge the last swillings of light.

I read, 'This is Kali Yuga, the Dark Age,
when all the great faiths are on the wane.'
Truth always brings assent, so I nod.

But then, from some tree in hesitant dusk
a small bird utters contradictions
of hope and despair . . .

'Evening Prayer', William Oxley[7]

This Advent, as indeed all Advents, comes within a context.
Each generation sees Advent and the faith with its own per-
spectives. Perhaps the reason why we so little value the true

significance of Advent is that we live in a world indifferent to the charms of God?

The poet has the same kind of questions. Are we in the Dark Age of faith? – and, if so, how can the hope and faith of Advent touch us? But, of course, all is not quite lost – it never is.

William Oxley experiences a moment – an epiphany – when he hears a small bird singing at dusk. Singing because it can, and it must. William begins to detect a small sign of hope – and faith – but it is fragile. As it is for most of us.

Advent asks us to consider our worldview – and ask ourselves questions like, why are we here and where are we heading? Are we prepared to change our worldview if we get good enough evidence that our assumptions are wrong? Would the Incarnation be enough to convince us of God's goodness?

Prayer

Father, thank you for this beautiful evening prayer. Help us to make time to stop and pray and to rest during our everyday lives. We identify with the poet's sense of despair mixed with hope. Father, I think we all have some of that about us. We pray today that there will be more hope than despair and that the balance will shift as we come to trust you more and more.

Help us to find hope in this Advent season in the world around us, in the creation you have made and in the tiny signals that all shall be well. Help us to stick with this Advent journey even when we're tempted to give up.

We crave hope and we know that you are the true source of hope and we pin our colours to you and what you have to offer.

Amen.

Teaching

Isaiah 25:6–10a
On this mountain the LORD Almighty will prepare a feast of rich food for all peoples, a banquet of aged wine – the best of meats and the finest of wines (v. 6).

Psalm 23
Matthew 15:29–37

Worldviews

My formative years were the 1970s. It's when I discovered music, sport, women, and I thought I'd worked out how the world worked. Unfortunately, that was based on an oil crisis, a miners' strike, a three-day week, power cuts, appalling haircuts, platform shoes and England failing to qualify for the football World Cup twice. By 1979, I had such a philosophically negative, almost stoic view of life that I was grateful for almost anything, and I was in danger of not believing that 'plenty' was possible.

Our world is one of plenty, but it is not built on a mentality of plenty. One of the fundamental building blocks of our world and our world view is the notion of 'scarcity'. *Scarcity* is fundamental to economics, because it drives the price of everything and decides how things get allocated. Scarcity says there is 'opportunity cost' – if you do one thing you cannot do another, and the greater the need for something the higher the cost. Not just gold, diamonds, or luxury jets, but basic food stuffs and hospital PPE. If people are starving, the price of food goes up, not down.

This has material consequences. Not only does it direct literally everything we do, but it affects the way we think. We think *scarcity*. For most of human history there has been an underlying fear that tomorrow, or next year, there won't be enough. This releases poor instinctive human behaviour, a 'poverty attitude' in the way we relate to our neighbour – remember our panic-buying phase?

The kingdom of God worldview is hard to accept, and most people do not accept it. The prophetic hope of kingdom faith is that 'the Lord Almighty will spread a wonderful feast for everyone around the world' (Isa. 25:6). Psalm 23 talks of having everything I need, green pastures, and a feast prepared for me in the presence of my foes. Matthew's gospel describes the kingdom in action, as Jesus heals the lame, the dumb and the blind, and feeds the hungry, by the thousand, with lots left over.

The great Advent call is to prepare our hearts to break out of this scarcity worldview. The assurance that there is always more than enough is both hope for tomorrow and a source of peace for today. My peace today means I can be a source of 'enough' for someone else.

Advent is a time when we question the mindset of the world – 'every man for himself' needs to give way to 'God is for every man!' The arrival of Christ means the 'kingdom of God is near' (Mark 1:15). Advent hope is not just about faith in a post-death nirvana, but the possibility that the kingdom of God can change hearts and behaviour now. This is the tiny hope the poet hears as he wonders if we are in a new dark age. The bird sings that perhaps all is not lost.

The 1970s did end. Since then for the whole of my life, I have wanted for nothing (Ps. 23:1).

Questions

- Do you think scarcity for plenty? How much of your world-view is imposed on you by the world itself?
- How might you take the hope of Advent and be a mes-senger of a new worldview among the people you know? How might you do that?

Thursday 1

What Is Love?

Shaped sounds that leave their pot pourri perfume
lingering in empty rooms,
melting into beeswax polish, curling
and swirling in mists of incense.
Folk tales, childhood incantations, favourite
scripture passages that have no need
to play on lips or echo in the chambers of the ear;
words repeated until their meaning drains away,
while sinking deeper, tender in the tinder of the heart;
and though their repetition conveys no information
can still surprise as echoes of hidden music
rise up through the mundane and familiar.
Words known more deeply than thought or memory,
creating in secret the context of identity:
important, trivial words that change the world,
like goodnight, and I love you.

'By Heart', Alwyn Marriage[8]

'I love you' is perhaps the most important thing that we can ever hear. If we do not hear it, or experience it, our lives are like deserts. Advent is all about 'I love you'. We are preparing ourselves for that moment when God demonstrated beyond all doubt that he is love and that we are precious to him. 'I love you', when delivered with sincerity, is the greatest life-changer of all.

We are so familiar with the stories at this time of year that they can become blunted and over-used. Story becomes cliché when spoken over and over again. But the poet wants to bring us back – to shake us up as we wonder at the power of 'I love you'. 'I love you' is like the echo of a hidden music, she tells us. When we aren't expecting it, it bubbles up and surprises us. That is exactly it. The world wasn't expecting the Christ. It was a secret that the angels were aware of. 'I love you' still has the power to transform us.

Prayer

Father, we thank you that at the heart of everything is love. To know that we are loved is our most basic need and to know that we are precious and that we matter is what helps us to get up in the morning and keep going.

Knowing that your love for us will never die lights up everything about our lives. We thank you for the dignity of human life, and we thank you that the world is changed by the action of your love and our love for neighbours and friends and for strangers.

Help us to let people know that they are loved by you and by us and not to be shy about doing so.

Amen.

Teaching

Isaiah 26:3
You will keep in perfect peace those whose minds are steadfast, because they trust in you.

Matthew 7:24–27
Psalm 118

'Trivial words that change the world, like goodnight, and I love you.'

'Goodnight and I love you' reminds me of going to bed when I was a child. I always slept well, because I went to bed feeling secure, and loved. If someone loves me, I mean really loves me, I know I can trust them. Love manifests itself in doing that which is best for the other. God loves us, we can trust him.

I am writing this in the middle of 2020 – in the time of the Covid-19 crisis. My pension plans and ISAs are not looking too hot and two of my family are furloughed, with two others enduring severe pay cuts. My house value has plummeted, and my paying tenant has vanished off the face of the earth. My church has been shut for eight weeks and no sign of it opening soon. A huge chunk of my personal trust, it seems, has rested in those things . . . small wonder I have never had 'perfect peace'.

God in his love has been stretching me. I wish he would not, but he does. The calamity of the Covid-19 crisis has spelled out to us that we place our hope and security in the wrong things – as Jesus warned, we build our houses on sand (Matt. 7:26). Our rich people trust in money and know nothing of trust in God, and our poor people have no money to trust in, so rely on debt. Our businesses run to the wire all the time, our banks lend to the limit, and our system relies so much on consumption that the earth cries out in agony. Our governments borrow too much and invest too little. Everything runs on empty, until the crisis.

This faith is all idolatry, and it will always eventually disappoint us. It may even kill us, for it has no power to save, only to pull the wool over our eyes. It certainly cannot keep us in perfect peace, only in perpetual neurosis! It is sand, easy to dig, but no basis for any kind of foundation.

The biblical hope is grounded in something the Hebrews called 'chesed' (pronounced *hessed*, but with phlegm!). This word describes the 'faithful love of God that endures for ever' (Ps. 118:1–4,29). It's sometimes translated as 'loving kindness' as the writer struggles to convey its rich, fathomless character. This, and this alone, is our faith and our hope – the rock on which we build.

If we pray 'Thy kingdom come', then we must make that inner leap of choosing no longer to trust in nation, party, power, finances and institutions, not even religion. God keeps in perfect peace those who trust in him – all else is allegiance to false gods.

Advent is a season of preparation, not a single day. That's because it takes time to prepare our minds for this Incarnation revolution. Building a house on the rock takes much longer, and it's hard work. You see, we can have these good material things, but we cannot have faith in them. Rock is hard to build on but will not let you down.

Questions

- What is your faith in? Can you trace your lack of perfect peace to building a house on sand?
- What are the barriers to trust in your life? Name them – it may help to disempower them just a little bit.

Friday 1

As Midnight Closes

The twelfth stroke makes its statement firm and clear.
As midnight closes I, too, draw a line
and through the darkness turn to face the day
more new, unspoilt and full of promises
than those I've chewed at, choked on
and spat out,
that now lie well behind me.

After such a year, what can we hope for?
What stake our lives on? Is there still a spark
that flickers through the darkness we have known?

Neither wishful thinking nor assurance;
poised between faith, coin of the Church,
and love, 'the best of all',

hope springs eternal,
leaps and bounds,
believes in bud, and leaf and flower,
and puppy-like joyfully welcomes friend and foe.

Against all recent evidence I throw
myself into the arms of hope
for the new year.

'Hope at Year's Turning', Alwyn Marriage[9]

After such a year, what can we hope for? It is a very good question indeed and one many of us have been asking. Never has there been a time when so many of us have felt our mental health to be so under threat. It is a combination of fear and loneliness and mourning the world as it was and may no longer ever be the same again. But the poet clings on to the indisputable fact that hope springs eternal.

Against all the evidence to the contrary, it is impossible to completely say goodbye to hope, and of course faith. Hope is like a tiny puppy that comes back again and again, unguarded and wanting to make friends with us – it cannot be chased off or discouraged. During Advent we wonder again about what the hope of the world really is. Can it really be about an out of the way place and a baby and family with the odds stacked against them?

The poet throws herself into the arms of hope, ready for the new year. What alternative do we really have? Hope, faith, love, are the currency of a life well lived and, as we think of that scene when God became one of us, it is good to let our hope spring forth again.

––––––––––––––––

Prayer

Father, after such a year we decide to throw ourselves into the arms of hope. We know now that hope is not something that is nice to have, but is something we need in the very depths of our soul. When everything seems to be grim and dark, help us to see that the light is coming; the light banishes the darkness and for this we pray.

At the end of the year we take stock and we begin to look forward to what the new year has in store for us. Holy Trinity, help us to see that you are with us on our journey into the new and that you have been with us all the way through the old. Let us take that tiny step away from despair and cynicism and towards the bursting forth of a new life and a new way and a new reality.

Amen.

––––––––––––––––

Teaching

Isaiah 29:17–end
In a very short time, will not Lebanon be turned into a fertile field and the fertile field seem like a forest? In that day the deaf will hear the words of the scroll, and out of gloom and darkness the eyes of the blind will see (vv. 17–18).

Psalm 27:1–4,16–17
Matthew 9:27–31

'After such a year, what can we hope for?'

The year 2020 was going to be my year (they all are, aren't they?). I had holidays planned, church planned, children's financial help all allocated, and resolutions all sorted. By mid-March it was seriously doubtful whether I had enough toilet roll in my world. Even writing this in lockdown, that juxtaposition still makes me laugh wryly in self-deprecation.

Soon this year will be over. We will be looking forward in hope to the year to come. We are still here, and we can take heart from the fact that, though this year may have disappointed us, we overcame it. Indeed, in some ways, we grew – our fruitful field is simply populated with different fruit.

More than that, the future is shaped in line with our hopes. But we cannot live by hope alone – it needs to have enough reality for us to believe in it.

Isaiah's vision of the future is beautifully described but written in terrible times. He writes amidst the siege of Jerusalem, in suffering, fear and privation. But he writes of fruitful fields, of the deaf hearing, and the blind seeing. More than this, those who intimidate, plot and exploit the poor will be no more. The prophet looks beyond the current crisis to proclaim hope; he lifts the fallen spirit. The gospel reading shows Jesus taking these words and making them literally and materially true. In this season of Advent, we are invited to prepare to think with joyful anticipation: '*After such a year, what can we hope for?*'

The answer is the kingdom of God. This is not a place or a country, it is not heaven and it is certainly not the church. It is a state of mind and place of faith and hope. It is a new economy, and a new reality. The faith and hope of the church, inaugurated in the Christmas story, is in this picture of liberation. It is liberation of the senses, from the inability to hear God, and the inability to see God. It is freedom from the tendency to operate against God, whether we realize it or not.

If we recognize Lebanon's fruitful fields as potentially right in front of us, we can hope for a much better year. This vision cannot be stapled onto the edge of a vision of life based on earthly things or simply trying harder. It is not attained through human power structures, but it can happen as people's ears are opened, and their eyes opened, and their lips released (Matt. 9:27–31). The world gets better, literally, if we get better, and we get better if we allow the kingdom of God to reign.

The hope of the future lies in the transformation of the present, through the healing of the human condition. If it never relates to now, then it is, as Marx said, the 'opiate of the masses', designed simply to pacify us. We need to believe in the perpetual miracle of God's reign in the transformed human heart, as we become conformed to the coming Christ (2 Cor. 3:18). When I see it that way, I can believe Isaiah's words to be literally true.

Questions

- Do you feel under siege? Knowing that many have gone through this tunnel, can you find hope in Isaiah's words?
- How might you re-engage with Christmas this year, to make some sort of breakthrough in your thinking? Is there someone who could help you?

Saturday 1

Waiting

Advent celebrates a waiting
hardly more than two took part in
and none bar prophets even dreamed beforehand:
it was just the songs of angels
bursting in on startled shepherds
made a larger audience aware
that waiting had been happening.

And elsewhen, less remarked, it still
continues while we work out who
has yet to venture to what Bethlehem
where labours end and revelation
overtakes whichever tradesmen
happen to be handy when deep longings
in denial are addressed.

Whether filled with hope or hollowed
by frustration's hungry edge,
on tiptoe is a better way of waiting
than playing with the condiments
in a cheap short-order diner
where all choices on or off the menu
are turning bad for lack of salt.

> 'What Are We Waiting For?', Michael
> Bartholomew-Biggs[10]

At various points in life, I have entered into a group-singing of *Why are we waiting?* Normally it would have been at school. It was never very serious.

Sometimes, though, we really do have an urgency with that question. Life suddenly feels perilous and we feel under threat. Then the waiting seems more serious. As the poet says, we are assailed by 'frustration's hungry edge.' There is a question that is even more profound than why are we waiting. The real question is, what are we waiting for? I think if we can get an answer to that question then our lives begin to make a great deal more sense.

The poet rather brilliantly helps us to understand the odd emptiness and loneliness of Advent. What are we waiting for? As this major question hangs in the air, almost no one at the time seemed to be part of the conversation. No one expected the question to be answered in the way it was, no one even saw that this was the great question of human existence. The world was unaware. Perhaps it still is. The poet has it right when he says that we have a deep longing for purpose. We need to make a choice to listen to the answers to questions like this. Advent is a strange mixture of the prosaic and the prophetic. Where do our labours end and revelation take hold?

The final stanza deserves rereading:

> Whether filled with hope or hollowed
> by frustration's hungry edge,
> on tiptoe is a better way of waiting
> than playing with the condiments
> in a cheap short-order diner
> where all choices on or off the menu
> are turning bad for lack of salt.

Wherever we are at, we tiptoe during the waiting game of Advent. We may be hopeful, frustrated or hollowed out, but we need to raise our eyes from, as the poet says, simply playing around with the simple business of trying to add just a little flavour to a poor dish. Why add useless flavour when what is on offer is nothing less than the real salt of human kindness and life? That is what we see during Advent, in the waiting and in the Incarnation.

So, let us continue to tiptoe through Advent. It is a particularly good image. If we tiptoe, we make sure we don't barge our way across others or miss something that might be important. Advent has an air of mystery, so we tread carefully – on tiptoe.

———————

Prayer

Father, help us to wait patiently in hope and expectation. Can you help us to tiptoe and not crush others? To be humble as we wait and to be people of peace and gentleness. We sometimes back away from the full majesty of what you have to offer – the glorious colours and taste of eternity – but in this time help us to approach you without fear and in expectation.

Amen.

———————

Teaching

Isaiah 30:18–21,23–36
Yet the LORD longs to be gracious to you; therefore he will rise up to show you compassion. For the LORD is a God of justice. Blessed are all who wait for him! (v. 18).

Psalm 146:4–9
Matthew 9:35 – 10:1,6–8

'Whether filled with hope or hollowed by frustration's hungry edge'

We are waiting. My childhood recollection of Advent is not as a time for spiritual preparation at all, other than the discipline of deferred gratification – waiting for Christmas Day made those presents even better, but I'd have had them on Advent Sunday if I'd been allowed. Today, I'd give a great deal for 'frustration's hungry edge', which I'm convinced is the secret of joy. Having all you want, all the time, right now, is a recipe for misery. I loathe Christmas decorations in October or even November, and Advent is too much like Christmas, spoiling the day when it arrives.

The interesting thing about Advent is that it makes us wait. Many of the Bible readings help us to understand what that waiting feels like and what it is for. The poet is interested in the waiting as well. He wonders about not just the waiting, but the way we wait. It matters that we wait well, that we are humble and don't go blundering around in frustration or despair or get side-tracked into trying to do God's work for him.

Yet so used are we to instant gratification and immediate answers that we have not learned to wait well.

Given the choice between making a choice that seems to give me what I want now and waiting for God to come through with something better, I will very frequently make the former (wrong) choice. I do it again and again and never seem to learn my lesson. The readymade solution in front of me is infinitely to be preferred to the possibility that God knows what he is doing, so I do it.

The background to the Isaiah passage is the worthless, disloyal treaty that Israel makes with Egypt for their own protection, instead of trusting in God and waiting for him. They choose a solution in front of their eyes, and available now, rather than the unseen solution that they would have to wait for.

God pleads with them to reject utterly the idols they have embraced and false deities in which they have placed their trust. I love it when the psalmist says, 'don't put your trust in powerful people . . . when their breathing stops they return to the earth' (Ps. 146:4). Can you see the fragility of it all? We habitually deposit ourselves in the care of ephemeral, transient and fundamentally unreliable things, institutions or people, because they are there and available. We can see them. They are easier to trust in.

Isaiah's tapestry of hope is awesome; coming to God is all about positive things. But there is a price, there is risk and there is discomfort. Not only do we need to wait, but our loyalties to human control (power, career, cash, whatever) are to be surrendered. The safety nets which we all build for ourselves need to be relegated or even discarded. We are all tempted to make treaties with Egypt, to place our security in something visible, tangible. We love a visible track record of materiality that we can see, assess and touch. We may need such things, but they are not the kingdom of God, and nor will they accomplish his goals. They breathe, then they stop breathing, and turn to dust.

Whatever I prefer to trust in, that is my real God. Advent, the waiting game, tells us something better, indeed best, is coming but not just yet. Wait, trust and then you will enjoy being asked to wholly trust in God to validate us and give us security. There is a gap between discarding those idols and seeing the reality of God's deliverance. It is an agonizing wait.

Between Isaiah and Jesus there was 700 years, and still we wait for the final coming of the kingdom. In between times, we wait and trust.

Questions

- Can you see in Advent that discipline of waiting? Do you agree with me about deferred gratification?
- Can you think of an example in your life now where you want God to act, but you have to wait? What happens in the waiting?

WEEK 2

Peace

Run down your bragging flags, they stain the sky.
And all their tattered flapping hurts the ears.
I know where all your gun emplacements lie.
I've known your every move for years and years.
Lay down your arms, your battered toys of war.
Each well-loved weapon is an open grave.
You think you know what you were fighting for:
You think you were all true and loyal and brave.
We thought the same. We fought for what was fair
And fine and pure and kind and strong and sweet.
We shot those fine ideals to thin air.
We left their bodies groaning at our feet.
All's fair in love and war. Each to the other,
We're what we need to be, my new-found brother.

'Advent 2', Jonathan Steffen[11]

At the heart of Advent is peace. It is a time to think about where we have been in conflict – with ourselves, with each other, with God – and begin to make good. It is no accident that, in *Silent Night*, the Christ child is enveloped in the sleep of heavenly peace. As the heavenly armies battle – Jesus finds a deep peace. In his life, when caught out in the middle of a deadly storm on the lake, he is found asleep aboard. It is not because he is uncaring or unconcerned. But he is peaceful, perhaps, because he knows the end of the story.

Advent is peaceful in a number of ways. It is the lull before the storm. The world waits for the birth of Jesus. When he is born all hell breaks loose, of course, with the murder of the innocents. But just now we are peaceful.

The poet has an epiphany – perhaps a very appropriate one for a time when the world has been hit by a pandemic and forced to stop. All that we thought was right and true has come into question. The getting, the competition, the trampling on others, the love of money and possessions. And then there is the demonization of others – of those who are different.

The wars and battles and selfishness, this Advent needs to be over. As we await the holy birth, we honour it by acknowledging our common humanity – we are all brothers and sisters. The Incarnation is conclusive proof that God loves us.

Sunday 2

Making Good

This house of broken words
of sleepers nailed
where barges passed an island
choked by mud
clogging up its garden,
where death has clawed its way
through mottled skin
where stones write hieroglyphics
gouged and marked,
where willows once stood tall
wept as they bowed
cut and sawn for indiscretions
witnessed,
where the river that comes and goes
has taken back its gifts
of salmon, bass and mollusc,
where the guest feels unwelcome

leaves admonished —
returns on uninvited days
to bring contrition to the wall,
plays his clarinet
to swans in the labour of their rest,
blows from one reed to many others,
delivers a forgotten language
to clean the shore.

'Sleepers', Sheila Aldous[12]

I like the idea that we throw our sins into the ocean of God's forgiveness. So often we harbour grudges even when we think we have accepted a sorry. At the next argument it all comes out again – the list of past wrongs and hurts. To quote the poet, our emotional lives are often an island clogged with mud – as we watch the barge of freedom pass by.

But in this season, we bring into the light the things we want, and need, to throw into the ocean of God's great forgiveness. The indiscretions and the embarrassments sink to the bottom, peacefully laid to rest. We never feel unwelcome with God. We are honoured guests. In this season we wait for him, with patience and with mature reflection – not self-condemnation.

This poem gives us another image for God's love and forgiveness. It is like a mighty river that in language we barely understand cleans the shore and leaves it fresh and new and beautiful. John the Baptist calls for repentance – clearing the shores of our troubled lives.

———————

Prayer

Father, give me the courage to make good with those I have wronged, but also not to persecute myself. Let me see myself as you see me. Let me be bold and trust you with my wrongs. Don't let me be defensive or full of pride.

Amen.

Teaching

Isaiah 40:1–11

Mark 1:1–8
I will send my messenger ahead of you, who will prepare your way – a voice of one calling in the wilderness, 'Prepare the way for the Lord, make straight paths for him' (vv. 2–3).

'. . . where barges passed an island, choked by mud, clogging up its garden'

Today's gospel quotes the Isaiah passage. The messenger was John the Baptist and he was quite a character, a very rare and unusual man. He seemed unsettled and overwrought. His job was to prepare the way, to unblock people's hearts and ears, which were 'choked by mud clogging up the garden'.

His unique qualities were those needed to break through the muddy conventions of the day. Breaking conventions is the engine of all change in the world, and John had one word for it – repentance, or '*metanoia*'.

Finding peace is sometimes, paradoxically, through a lack of peace, an internal challenge, a call to 'repent'. Repentance is turning away from the dross, the mud of our lives and turning towards God. It is the fresh start we all need, but that takes us being honest with God. The poet understands that making good is part of our journey to adulthood and wholeness. Repentance and peace go together. John the Baptist understood this. But it can be unsettling, a time of upheaval.

Peace is often the fruit of a short season of conflict. I find that times of dissonance, or discomfort, are often the only way that God can stimulate me to change things. Confrontation and peace, strangely, are sometimes close allies; the mud needs to be confronted with a choice to scrub it clean and start afresh.

The choice costs though. For me it entails some pain because it often means putting something right, or confessing something, or sacrificing something, or just admitting I was wrong.

It must have been costly for John too. He was born into the priestly temple community, the son of parents who were rich and privileged compared to most other people. He was willing to set all that aside to establish his own ministry, gaining some integrity in poverty (his dwelling place, his clothing, his locusts and wild honey). The real humility though, and probably the real internal conflict, was the realization that his own ministry didn't matter. His part in the narrative was to step aside completely at the right moment.

The path of peace is expensive. There is loss. Sometimes we cannot scrub the muddy clothes clean, we need to discard them altogether. John knew he had to empty himself, say goodbye to much that life might otherwise have offered, and decline to start building his own career (John 3:30). Jesus' first disciples were disciples that John gave away (John 1:29–34). John's mission was to point beyond himself to that man over there, the one coming that I'm not even worthy to serve, the lamb who takes away the sin of the world, including mine. The poet also wants to get beyond herself, to somewhere new and fresh.

That is a pattern we should emulate if we want the same peace and assurance that John had. A lack of peace often stems from the insecurity inherent in building your own show. I have learned that building a little self-centric castle to try and build a peaceful life is counterproductive. I have found in middle age that if I decrease and allow him (and others) to increase, finally I find my peace.

Questions

- Where in your life do changes and sacrifices need to be made in order to relieve the sense of siege?
- Is life all about building your own show? Is that what God wants?

Monday 2

What Is the Path?

I am under vows to you, my God;
   I will present my thank-offerings to you.
For you have delivered me from death
   and my feet from stumbling,
that I may walk before God
   in the light of life.

Psalm 56:12–13

Darkness and light are constant themes during Advent. It is really rare in our country to experience true darkness. Light pollution has seen to that. But just sometimes we do get a glimpse of real darkness.

One Christmas, I was up with my family in North Dalton, East Yorkshire. It is a beautiful village on the High Wold. It just has a pub and a few cottages and is my idea of heaven. It helped that my relatives owned the pub. One night I woke up at about 2 a.m. and couldn't find the light. It was pitch black and I couldn't even see my hand in front of me. Even though I was in my forties I felt scared. The darkness makes us vulnerable and we feel like children again.

So, the promise of light defeating darkness is a strong one – a reassuring one.

As we build to Advent, anticipate it, we are encouraged to be thankful. But what should we be thankful for? I start each day saying thanks to God and I tend to come up with the same list most days – I am thankful for my family, my church, my health, that I went to university and that I have had an interesting life. The psalmist, too, knows that gratitude is the right attitude. He relates that God has saved him from death – that he has been saved.

It is a good poem – a good prayer. But this kind of gratitude comes from one place. We need to know that we need saving – from ourselves, from sin, from all that operates against the good and faithful life. In this week of Advent, we wonder about peace – something very hard to come by. The psalmist pushes us to a more eternal perspective – peace comes not from meditation or seeking pleasure, but from gratitude and knowing that God saves. That's what he is in the business of.

The boy, Jesus, born away from his home village, in difficult circumstances, is the emblem of that heavenly peace. On this and every silent night, God is in no hurry and is never flustered. Deep peace is on offer, if only we take the time to grasp it. The metaphor of the path is useful. We are travelling on one, and for each of us the ground can sometimes seem treacherous.

———————

Prayer

Father, I often feel as though I am stumbling. But I so want to be right with you and to follow the glorious path of light. Help me when I fall and let me start again each day of my life. As St Benedict said, 'Always, we begin again'.

Amen.

———————

Teaching

Psalm 85:7–end
I will listen to what God the LORD says; he promises peace to his people, his faithful servants – but let them not turn to folly. Surely his salvation is near those who fear him, that his glory may dwell in our land (vv. 8–9).

Luke 5:7–26

In Luke 5 Jesus heals a paralysed man. This healing is unique in the length to which the man's friends go to get him in front of Jesus. It is such an unlikely scenario that I believe it must have happened exactly as described. His friends climb onto the roof, strip the tiles and lower him down through it – it is the only way to get him in. They show great faith and push past the religious people to get to Jesus. They know that their friend is living a kind of death and they want to put him back on the path to wholeness and restoration.

Jesus sees not just the need, but the real inner desire, and heals him with the words 'Son, your sins are forgiven'. He not only heals him; he grants him peace.

The problem with our sin is not the breaking of the rule, whatever the rule is (it was against the rules to dismantle a guy's roof!). Sin is not rules; it is both cause and symptom of a lack of peace. It is essentially alienation – a division that springs up between us and God, between us and creation, between us and others whom we mistreat, and between us and ourselves as we grapple with self-guilt and shame. Forgiveness is a four-fold reconciliation, a most wonderful thing. 'Son, your sins are forgiven' is a blessing of peace, not just a judicial verdict.

Paul writes of it in a stunning way: 'through him God was pleased to reconcile to himself all things, whether on earth or in heaven, by making peace . . . And you who were once estranged and hostile in mind, doing evil deeds, he has now reconciled in his fleshly body' (Col. 1:20–22, NRSVA).

The picture the Bible paints is that we are unavoidably alien-ated from God because we follow our own ways. God has granted us sovereignty over our own lives, and we tend to misuse that, mostly because we are tribal, nationalistic and selfish. Paul even describes us as 'enemies of God' in this alienated state.

The psalmist at the start of this day understood alienation – being apart from God. He talks about having stumbled and been close to death. Feeling away from God feels like a kind of death. Mother Teresa had just this long-dark night of the soul. She felt alienated from God for decades. What did she do? She carried on doing God's work.

President Abraham Lincoln once famously declared: 'I destroy my enemies by making them my friends.' That is the language of reconciliation, making things right by making people right with each other. That is the wonderful way God works, and its fruit is peace. Advent is the announcement, the proclamation, that God is coming to destroy his enemies by making them his friends.

Questions

- In what ways does 'your sins are forgiven' mean more than just letting you off the things you have done wrong? Is there an even bigger picture?
- How much more powerful is reconciliation than just forgiveness?

Tuesday 2

Peace When We Can't Settle

There are days
When I cannot paint angels
Or devils
Or Jesus
Or Mary
Or even my favourite saint, Francis;
There are days when I have to paint
Horses, and asses, and oxen, and sheep.

On such days, I remind myself
That Jesus is the Lamb of God;
And I thank the Lord
For making sheep
So extremely difficult to paint well.

'School of Giotto', Jonathan Steffen[13]

The poet is having problems settling into his normal artistic routine. There are days, he tells us, when he can't really bring himself to think about his faith. I understand this completely. Sometimes I get the feeling that I would just like to do normal things and enjoy the world around me without thinking too much. I need a rest from all things holy.

Jonathan finds there are days when he can't paint angels or anything else relating to his religious life. Sometimes, religion doesn't make us feel peaceful, which is of course all to do with us and not at all to do with God.

The poet does find a way out. On the days when he isn't feeling peaceful, he paints horses and sheep and the like. These creatures that we share our world with can be very calming and painting them can help us to be deeply peaceful not just in our work but in our life as well. I don't paint, but I do take great pleasure from looking at the world around me; the birds in the garden, the trees and the clouds. Creation speaks peace into our lives, not least because we see the Creator in it.

On these days when the poet is stuck painting sheep, he reminds himself that Jesus is the Lamb of God, which is perhaps the most beautiful image for God in the whole of Scripture. Thinking of Christ as the Lamb brings out great thankfulness more generally for our animal friends. The poet is thankful the sheep are quite difficult to paint, drawing a comparison with the painting of anything and the painting of our own faith.

Peace is sometimes hard-won – brushstroke by brushstroke.

_____

Prayer

Father, I sometimes feel unsettled and anxious. I can't settle
and am easily distracted. I want to have focus and do the
right thing, but then I can't see myself doing it. Let me rest
when I need to rest and, in this season, to see you at work
even when I am doing nothing.

Amen.

———————————

Teaching

Isaiah 40:1–11
Psalm 96:1,10–end

Matthew 18:12–14
If a man owns a hundred sheep, and one of them wan-
ders away, will he not leave the ninety-nine on the hills
and go to look for the one that wandered off? And if
he finds it, truly I tell you, he is happier about that one
sheep than about the ninety-nine that did not wander
off. In the same way your Father in heaven is not willing
that any of these little ones should perish.

'There are days when I cannot paint angels . . .'

I am supposed to have faith, and through faith have courage,
and through courage have peace. Sometimes I can't do it.

Religious imagery, language and attempted comfort make it worse, not better. The basic reason is, when I feel that way, I feel accused by my own lack of virtue. I'm not supposed to have anxiety: I'm a Christian – obviously not a very good one . . . and so it goes.

The fact is, I do not much like threat and danger. Threat brings a natural defensiveness in me. It may be a material threat, or just an accusation or a threat to my pride, but I do not necessarily deal with it too well. When feeling secure I am perfectly able to be quite a nice person, but corner me and I fight. What I need in those situations is someone not to offer me comfort, but to make me feel safe. By safe, I mean being allowed to be vulnerable without coming to actual harm.

It is part of the human condition to feel threatened even by God himself. The God of mere human religion becomes our accuser. Interestingly, that is what 'Satan' means – accuser. Our very faith, sometimes emphasizing our guilt and unworthiness, makes us feel insecure, instead of safe. We know we are not right, and we know we have a lot to answer for. It is natural then to see God as a threat.

Isaiah is instructed to 'Comfort my people' (Isa. 40:1).

The birth of Jesus is God's affirmation of flesh; it is comfort and peace. Its great central message is that, when all else is stripped away, when the grass withers and the flowers fade, God endorses humanity. He approves of flesh and the human form. Ultimately, we must eventually die like all living things, but we will not 'perish' because we are his.

The great peace of God is that, through Christ, we are held for all eternity, long past the physical withering of our own earthly bit of grass. If we can accept this, we will feel secure. If we can feel secure and affirmed despite the inner voice, I'm convinced we will behave differently. If we carry this peace within us, then we can be a blessing to others.

When Jesus is born, the angels meet the shepherds in the fields and cry out, 'Glory to God in the highest heaven, and on earth peace'. The peace and triumph of the Incarnation points beyond ourselves and points to the fact that we have acceptance in God; indeed, we are embraced by him as children.

The poet finds peace through ditching an obsession with religion. He instead focuses on something more everyday. Sometimes we need a break from the false God we create. We are simple humans and the awe and power of God can be overwhelming. The poet leaves behind the grown-up subjects of his work (the devil, Mary, etc.) and does something childlike. He paints sheep.

Questions

- What do you feel God is accusing you of? Could you talk to him about it?
- Do you see the Incarnation as God's judgement, or God's salvation?

Wednesday 2

It Is Hard to Describe the Colours

Hard to describe the colours of this winter landscape.
They are bleached by the milky veil of freezing air
And anyway, it is so cold one can barely think.
But if I strive, I can discern
Thin russets and dull olives and gun-metal greys
Among the naked trees;
I can see how the snow on the hilltops
Is tinged with pale blue
And the snow by the roadsides
Is tinged with khaki.
Here and there a patch of bracken
Huddles in the blankness like a group of shaggy ponies.
Three crows perch on the top of an oak tree,
The only true black in the scene.
And the sky . . .
The sky is a colour that hovers between grey and white,
The colour of the promise of more snow to come.

From the colour, I cannot say when it will come.
Nor can I say when I will see you again.
But this is a winter scene,
And the light is already starting to fade,
And it is far too cold for any more words now.

'Winter Landscape', Jonathan Steffen[14]

It does no harm to return for a dose of realism. It is cold outside, and the weather is grim. The sky is grey and white and we long for a bit of colour. Sometimes we get the gift – or should that be mixed blessing? – of snow.

When the skies are grey and it is cold I find that I tend to go into my shell. As a boy, I used to dream of emigrating to America and living there in California. I wanted somewhere where the sun shone, and the living was good. I am now glad that I didn't act on my dream. How would we appreciate the sun and the warmth if we did not experience the cold and grey?

Somehow, I get the sense that all of creation was waiting for the change that Christ bursting into the world delivered. The sun, moon and stars, all were preparing. As were the animals and plants and trees.

———————————

Prayer

Father, in this Advent help me to know that the whole of creation was preparing for the great event to come. Help me to see God in all that is around me and to enjoy the animals and birds and trees and clouds. Let me know that the cold weather is only temporary. In my prayers help me to be silent when I need to be and to let you be all around me.

Amen.

Teaching

> *Isaiah 40:25–end*
> 'To whom will you compare me? Or who is my equal?' says the Holy One. Lift up your eyes and look to the heavens: who created all these? (v. 25–26).

> *Psalm 103:8–13*
> *Matthew 11:28–end*

'The sky is a colour that hovers between grey and white.' Pretty soon in winter, it will become inky black, darker than any summer sky. In that inky black, the astronomer thrives because it is in that intense darkness that the stars can be seen. Engulfed by darkness, and millions of years away (not just miles), they still shine. They are sufficient for some people to navigate by and the biblical testimony to God's great majesty. In that extreme darkness, the light is even more visible.

Our earthly existence is a kaleidoscope. It is not all sweetness and light, and sometimes the greatest things are discovered in the realism of the hardest things. One thing is for sure – escapism and pretence don't really work. The poet has reached just such a hard place. The gun-metal skies and the cold have got deep into his soul. Where to from here? If into darkness, then he will need the light of the stars.

Isaiah points us to the stars as a testimony to God. Jesus makes it personal: 'Come to me, all you who are weary and burdened, and I will give you rest.' The combination of these readings invites us once more to relate to the God of the infinite as the God of the intimate. This could be the medicine the poet needs on a cold winter's day.

The testimony of the stars always fascinates me. I believe the heavens proclaim the glory of the Lord (Ps. 19:1). The universe is a reality – the earth is not flat, not young, and by no means the centre of everything. This is the testimony of 'general revelation'; it complements Scripture, makes us work hard for Scripture's real, lasting meaning, and Scripture honours it. Look to the stars and you will see God's calling card.

General revelation is utterly vast. There are a billion stars in the one galaxy that we inhabit, the Milky Way. There are 200 billion such galaxies (and counting: some now say trillions).

It is literally true that the stars outnumber the grains of sand on the beaches of the world. When I read that I simply could not believe it. So, I did some more Googling. The bottom line is, if the low-end estimate for the number of stars matches the high-end estimate for the number of grains of sand, the two numbers equate (still staggering!). But in all likelihood, there are five to ten times more stars than there are grains of sand on all the world's beaches. That, to me, is showing off, but it means I can trust God with my soul, even on a grey metal sky day tending to blackness.

The dark, dark days of Covid-19 had a hidden blessing of sacred illumination; I learned what really mattered. The sovereignty of God was easier to see, and my own weakness more apparent.

The God and the Christ that stands outside that creation, and freely enters into it, has knitted you in your mother's womb (Ps. 139), and knows the very hairs on your head (Luke 12:7).

Questions

- Does the actual universe call your faith into question, or does it strengthen it?
- Consider the juxtaposition of the vast cosmos and God's care for you as one mortal human being. Can the darkness sometimes be a help in seeing what is significant?

Thursday 2

How We See the World

Among the gods there is none like you, Lord;
no deeds can compare with yours.

Psalm 86:8

The Psalmist wants us to think about our worldview. We all have one. We see the world through a particular lens, made up of a set of assumptions about how the world works and how we operate in it. There are so many worldviews to choose from.

In the ancient world, for instance, there was epicureanism – eat, drink and be merry for tomorrow we might die. We'd probably call it hedonism. Or there was stoicism – life frequently sucks, get used to it and expect nothing else. These days we are in the midst of postmodernism – there is no such thing as ultimate truth – we each have our own truths. If it is true for you, then however odd, that is your truth.

But the Christian faith and the progress through Advent ask us to consider what is true truth? The psalmist asserts that there is no other god like God. That God is behind all of creation – all the great deeds. Of course, it is easy to get a rather narrow picture of the God who does stuff, who rules everything. But Advent asks us to wonder what a great deed looks like.

The messy birth in an unglamorous house in the middle of nowhere doesn't look like a great deed at all. It looks like folly. If God were going to come – why not come as a royal prince, full of might? If our worldview can encompass a view of the humble and domestic God, then it might help us to be more humble in turn.

———————

Prayer

Father, we claim you as the ultimate truth. We know that there are many truths in this world but that in the final analysis the only truth that counts is your grace in love. Help us to know that you are close and that you do not disdain our ordinary lives. Help us not to look down on people who don't believe the same things we do.

Amen.

———————

Teaching

Isaiah 41:13–20
Psalm 145

Matthew 11:11–15
For all the Prophets and the Law prophesied until John. And if you are willing to accept it, he is the Elijah who was to come. Whoever has ears, let them hear (vv. 13–15).

We are still thinking about worldview. Just what shaped lens do we have right in front of our eyes? It determines how we see everything and how we hear God. Just to mix metaphors horribly, our eyes make us deaf.

Jesus highlights the people's inability to understand what the Scriptures had been plainly saying for centuries. Their preferred world was pulled over their eyes. They believed 'in the Scriptures' but had them wrong. John was great, not because of his own personal 'merits', but because he understood the Scriptures, read them right and was preparing the way for Jesus by bringing people to repentance.

John was announcing the fulfilment of the prophecies in Isaiah. God had them by the right hand, the poor and needy would have their thirst quenched, and the joy of the Lord would fill them to overflowing. Some of his hearers heard, many could not understand it. The actual world wasn't like that, surely? That view of God is just too good to be true.

Maybe that's what we need to reflect on. The psalmist who glories in God's mighty deeds is telling deep truth, but only part of it. God is mighty, but we are weak and needy and sometimes get lost. It is no coincidence that Jesus casts himself as the shepherd going after the confused and stubborn sheep.

What causes this blindness and uncomprehension in our lives? For me, it is that I lack the peace to hear the voice of God. This is because my life is a scramble from one worry to the next. Most are rather formless worries concerning the near or mid-term future. Winston Churchill, in reflective mood, wrote: 'When I look back on all these worries, I remember the story of the old man who said on his deathbed that he had had a lot of trouble in his life, most of which had never happened.'

We have real troubles, but the worst ones are those that never happen – ask anyone with anxiety issues, the worldview of what might happen (and what people might say!) is totally destructive. The absence of peace leads to an inability to hear and understand, and more 'mind fog'. We are transfixed by enemies in front of our face and cannot see God standing a few feet further on. I'm getting anxious just writing this!

There is another worldview, perceived by the prophets of whom John was the last. The Advent journey invites you to reset this button, to break into the vicious circle and remind yourself of the promise of God fulfilled in Christ. Do not fear, I'm coming, says the Lord.

Questions

- Why not audit your major anxieties? How many of them have actually materialized (I acknowledge that some might have, of course)?
- Also audit your walk with God. How has he been faithful, even if you do not have everything you want?

Friday 2

Forgiveness

I notice bindweed growing through the borders
remember a chore never over
however much I dig it, pull it,
over and again.

Forgiveness too –
I think I've done it
then I come across
more shoots already strangling
plants I want to thrive.

These crossings out for instance –
easy to take a pencil
strike through a word, a line
silence a voice
that deals in doubt

or when certain paths cross –
the body's memory of shock
as old emotions burst their banks

so once more, I'm getting out my spade
digging at shoots
I don't want to give soil-room
doing the work
weeding my own patch

over and again.

'Spadework', Jennie Osborne[15]

I am not very good at spadework. I used to go and help my dad on his allotment. I seemed to lose interest whenever it was my time to get digging. Digging takes effort and you are never quite sure what you will dig up. On the allotment it was often a case of digging up hard compacted clay or the odd tin can.

But I am called as a Christian to do some spadework – especially in Advent. It is a time, an opportunity, to make good, and that takes some courage.

When I became a Christian, I made a list of the people I felt I had wronged in my life (it wasn't a very long list!). I then rang each of them to apologize. It was a salutary experience, but I am glad that I did it.

The poet beautifully captures the need for spadework and what it takes to do it. We all need to take out our spades and dig and keep digging. We need to purge the things we don't want to grow.

———————————

Prayer

Father, help me to have the courage to do the spadework – not wallowing in all that is wrong, but as a way of making a fresh start. Help us to know that this is an ongoing part of the adult life and not to be feared.

Amen.

———————————

Teaching

Isaiah 48:17–19
'I am the LORD your God, who teaches you what is best for you, who directs you in the way you should go. If only you had paid attention to my commands, your peace would have been like a river, your well-being like the waves of the sea.'

I, like most people reading this, had a childhood that was characterized by those words: 'if only you'd listened'. There were quite a few instances of this. It really is part of the human condition to think that we know better. I used to make scale models, which involved the use of rather noxious substances such as glue, paint and thinner. I received copious advice on how to manage these hazards, but that all took time and I just wanted to get on with it. One almighty mess later, those inevitable words would come – 'if only you'd listened'.

Repentance, forgiveness, and the making good of relationships are central to the story of God and his people. What God is saying here, through Isaiah, is that the trouble they were in was of their own making, not of his angry judgement, but that he allows this tribulation because 'he teaches you for your own good'. We need to repent because we don't listen in advance. I guess it will always be so.

That means the 'spadework' needs to be done and redone, and all the time. Our tendency to wander, learn things the hard way, and need to return to God via pathways of tears and struggle, are like the bindweed in the garden. We think we have dealt with it, and then it comes back.

God's so-called 'judgement' is often simply 'consequence', but in his hands, is restorative. It always has the objective of making good. Despite the fact we do not pay attention, and even though we will do it again, God desires to make us turn back to him. This was true of Israel constantly, and it is true of us.

Advent, like Lent, points us to an event that focuses the mind. It is not 'ordinary time', it has a focus. That focus can act as the reminder to set our inner house in order, both to repent and to forgive. It is a great time to engage in the business of making good. It is a great time to reach out to others, maybe those we have lost touch with, and a great time to make up with people.

Allowing ourselves to be taught by God and to be content takes great surrender. It really is not easy at all. It is the act of lifting our own agenda and pictures of self-worth to God and saying, as I had to, 'Dad, this is a mess, can you fix it?' As a child I said it many times, and as a father, I lost count of the number of times I was asked the same thing.

Listening of course requires one critical decision – the decision to actually stop talking for a while. Advent can offer us a focused time of listening – we do not need to be constantly doing or talking. Part of that listening might be for the cries of the oppressed, broken and poor. If we listened to that, we might be filled with compassion. We must beware not to privatize faith – to make it just a matter of me and God and what I can get out of it. We are called to listen to the broken and be the people they feel safe telling their stories to.

Questions

- Where do you need to stop, pause and listen to God's counsel? Are you trusting in something that is going to let you down?
- If you have messed up, where is the learning? Can you and God together redeem the situation?

Saturday 2

Always the Same Old Silence

Always the same old silence
And the same old,
Always different,
Northern light.
Always the same old smell
Of dried-out clay
And dried-out paint
And dried-out ideas.
That brush I haven't touched in years.
That palette knife remains my favourite.
So many pencils sharpened in hope . . .
My workbench is flecked with colours
That have not become anything at all
While ceasing to be themselves.
Here is a brownish smear
That was once Vermilion.
There is a spattering of grey

That was once Ultramarine.
And, in their tubes,
Resplendent with their unique names,
The still-virgin paints are waiting.
A Rose Madder
That is quite innocent of the world.
A Sap Green
That does not even know that it is Sap Green.
And here am I,
Surveying the debris of so many years
And reflecting on so many possibilities,
Available, as always,
Just in case an angel
Should pass through my north-facing window
And perch for one instant on my workbench,
Its wings ablaze with colours
For which only God knows the names.

'Studio', Jonathan Steffen[16]

I have the feeling that joy is hard-won. That has been the experience of my life. Amid the winter gloom it is easy to feel gloomy as well. But Advent declares a joy that did and will continue to change the world.

The poet is feeling dried up and the old paints and brushes remind him of this. He wants to be creative, but it isn't happening. He sees the ghosts of projects that have never got off the ground. Each fleck of paint is a masterpiece that never left the workbench. Despite the colours, the poet's world is rather black and white. Or maybe it is the poet's past life that looks like a failure – a failure of the imagination with a deficit of joy.

But all is not lost, which is, in itself, a great Advent message. The poet suddenly has a beautiful thought and one that lights him up with true colour, and contradicts his sense of futility.

His creativity is worth it, just in case an angel lands for a moment with his wings ablaze with a colour that only God can name. That blazing is joy, pure joy, and that is why we so anticipate the birth of the King of Joy.

Prayer

Father, sometimes the path to joy seems impossible and difficult. Sometimes all we can do is put the right preparations in place and hope that joy might come our way. In the barren and difficult times, give us hope and heart. In this Advent season let us know that, even if we are feeling flat and empty, there is joy on the way and that joy cannot be turned aside from. Let us be filled with sudden, wild and unexpected hope and joy. We wish this on all around us; friend and foe alike.

Amen.

Teaching

2 Kings 2:9–12

Psalm 80
Restore us, O God; make your face shine on us, that we may be saved (v. 3).

Matthew 17:10–13

'Always the same old silence, and the same old, always different, northern light'

We have a north-facing garden. The greatest challenge I face in making things grow and display colour there is *aspect*. The soil is rich and nutritious, if a little heavy, and I can water things as much as I like, but I cannot make it brighter. Without sufficient light, I can't make colourful flowers grow; they lack the health and vigour that is required, because the sun does not shine on them enough.

Colour is only reflected light. I love references in the Bible to the shining face of the Lord, as in the great priestly blessing of Numbers 6 which says, 'The LORD bless you and keep you; the LORD make his face shine on you'. The feeling of God's face shining on me is a healing one, a sense of affirmation and peace.

The other two passages talk about Elijah being taken up to heaven and returning metaphorically as John the Baptist, fulfilling a great prophecy in Malachi 4:2, which in turn contains this fantastic promise of more light, the return of 'the sun of righteousness . . . with healing in its rays.'

John the Baptist is the linking prophet between the Old Testament promise and the fulfilment we see in Jesus. It is portrayed as light coming into darkness. Advent is the time when we prepare both minds and hearts to see this. We are all like north-facing gardens – we have the potential to thrive, but we need God's face to shine upon us. When God's face shines on us the fruit of that light is health and healing. We are restored to what we should be.

The light heals, and healing is peace. Our inner conflicts are resolved and calmed; the immune system can rest from its work and the nerve cells stop transmitting their pain signals. If our institutions, politics and systems are healed, then our corporate body can be at peace as well. If we reject the chance, we remain in our conflicted, un-healed state, and the great day of the Lord passes us by. Like the poet, we need to be on the look-out for shards of hope and joy.

The average object reflects 18 per cent of the light that lands on it. The rest it absorbs. That is all you see, just 18 per cent. But consider the vast array of colours that it reveals. All our earthly beauty is released by just a small percentage of reflected light.

If I could reflect 18 per cent of the light that God sends on me, I'd be changing the world.

Questions

- Have you really read the Old Testament, or have you read what others have said about it?
- Do you need healing and restoration? Can you sense the face of the Lord shining? What might that mean for you?

WEEK 3

Joy

The waters of my heart are dark and deep
And chill and timeless beyond human knowing;
And even I cannot guess what's asleep
And what is stirring where the murk is flowing.
A mystery to themselves, they hold a world
Of hours and days and nights and months and years –
Now tightly intertwined, and now unfurled
To drift on wilful waves of hopes and fears.
Yet in the towering autumn of my days,
Against a disappearing disc of sun,
With half the world asleep and half ablaze,
And so much of my lifetime's journey done,
Hopes rise like geese within this broken breast
And lift in one clear delta for the west.

'Advent 3', Jonathan Steffen[17]

We head back to the strange hinterlands of hope and its close cousin, joy. Like the poet, I too am in the autumn of my days. Perhaps, like all thinking people, I can be a mystery to myself. Consciousness is a great mystery. Where on earth did it come from? Is it possible that enzymes and chemical formulations that began in the primeval sludge could become a creature able to recognize itself and all its imperfections and dilemmas?

As the sun goes down, the poet is struck by a kind of awe at the world. The sun is a ball of fire. Half the world sleeps while the other half wakes. We have all had many hopes dashed. But what if, even late in life, there is still one great hope? That we might rise like wild geese, flying in formation towards the west?

It is a striking image. The pause of Advent is a pause of great hope. Like those geese we fly towards hope – the great hope that God is in the flying with us, in the formation of incomplete people, wondering what to do with their brokenness.

Sunday 3

Defend Yourself, God

Rise up, O God, and defend your cause;
remember how fools mock you all day long.

Psalm 74:22

Again, the psalmist is calling God to action. People mock God – they still do. Mockery is very hard to take, of course. Outright hostility we can deal with; but mockery is another matter, often because it plays on our worst fears. Christ himself was mocked by the Roman soldiers as he faced his death. It must have been a bitter pill.

Advent is the time when the tables begin to turn. God had been silent for centuries and the people of God were feeling anxious about it. What if he had simply shut up shop? The silence of God is difficult for us all.

In Advent the wheels are beginning to turn, although almost no one at the time knew it. They were living their normal lives, just getting on and getting by. Life was full of frustrations, especially living under occupation. There was a pent-up longing for God to come and deliver his people.

But quietly and amid the stirrings of everyday life, God was doing something. A teenage girl and her husband were expecting a child. Some obscure wise men were following a star. But elsewhere all was normal.

Viewed from the perspective of might and power, Advent and Christmas are supremely foolish. Why would God risk anything on us humans? Why would he risk mockery? Why would he risk being a helpless babe in perilous circumstances?

Good sense says that God should have arrived with a trumpet fanfare of a million angels. That he should have taken residence here in all his glory, striking down his enemies and establishing a time of peace. But no, he does the opposite and in these quiet days as we lead up to the birth of Christ, we must ponder the foolishness of God and see that as part of his glory.

The psalmist asks God to 'remember how fools mock you all day long'. But I wonder if God is too busy working on our behalf to be bothered with that. Being born a human is not sensible at all. People will continue to mock.

Advent asks us to pause and wonder if we too might be more foolish and less sensible. And perhaps when the psalmist called upon God to defend himself, he had no idea how de-fenceless God would be.

———————————

Prayer

Father, we live in a time when faith is mocked. Many people think that we are foolish, and our faith is based on nothing at all. When we are mocked, it pains us to think that you are mocked as well. That's why the cross is so difficult for us to comprehend. In all your glory you were prepared to be mocked. But in this Advent season we pray for many to know your love, mercy and grace.

Amen.

———————————

Teaching

Isaiah 61:1–2a,10–11
The Spirit of the Sovereign LORD is on me, because the Lord has anointed me to proclaim good news to the poor (v. 1).

Advent is the time when the tables begin to turn. This pas-sage in Isaiah has special significance because in Luke 4 Jesus declares: 'Today this scripture is fulfilled in your hearing.'

There is coming a progressive liberation, and it comes from the proclamation of good news.

The Bible is richly metaphorical, which has the great advantage that its essence can be transported from the time and place it was written and be applicable to all people, in all places, in all ages. The language of Isaiah seems to me to be a picture painted in words, alluding to a beautiful future reality. The prophetic picture of Christmas in the Old Testament is metaphorical; the fulfilment is in flesh, so it is real, and the joy of it is that it applies everywhere. But to say that this picture in Isaiah is not literal is not to say that it is meaningless, and certainly not abstract.

Yet it is a worldview that would have been quietly mocked in the context of its time. In practice, not even the Jews honoured the poor in the way that God does. They, too, regarded riches and power as signs of God's favour, and poverty and sickness as a sign of his disfavour. It's odd, because no parts of the Scripture say that; it seems to be an inbuilt human thing to think that way. The good news is that God displays a bias, always and everywhere, for those that 'lack'.

God, in sending Jesus, fulfils what Isaiah promised 700 years before. God has declared himself to be the good news. The good news is not a theological system, it is a person, the personification of God. And, as it turns out, God is . . . good news. God is good news for the poor, the oppressed and the broken-hearted.

Sometimes we need to take this at face value and work out how it plays out in practice for us. So, when Isaiah proclaims good news to the oppressed, to bind up the broken-hearted, and when Jesus echoes this in his Nazareth manifesto in Luke 4, we have to work out how or why it remains unfulfilled. How does the Incarnation mean the good news that Isaiah predicted? It certainly seems much more precarious than the psalmist suggested it would be.

That is partly fulfilled in the world to come but we must not leave it there and hope for the best. We need to become the outworking of that good news, otherwise it really is not good news at all. We do this in obedience to Jesus and confident that it represents the 'good news'. I think Jesus wants us to be transformed so that we can bring joy into the 'now'. It is the mission of the church not to point people to an unprovable future, but to bring joy into the present.

We do that by proclaiming Isaiah's great vision: everyone is included, everyone is forgiven and made new, and true happiness is found in each other, not in materialism and wealth.

And that is literally true. It's more than a hope, more than pie in the sky. It is what the kingdom should look like right now. This is a joyful statement, because it might not have been. It could have been true that God did not care for the poor or bind up the broken hearts.

But because he does, and Jesus shows he does, we can find joy in human existence because of where it is heading and what the journey might bring.

Questions

- How far do you think we can have heaven now? What does this say about the 'kingdom of God'?
- What good news do you really need? What imprisonment and poverty do you feel bound by?

Monday 3

The Cruellest Month

On the shortest day,
I walk, reading the birds
Starlings massed on black trees are hieroglyphs
telling the loss of the sun

Extract from 'December', Victoria Field[18]

T. S. Eliot wrote that April was the cruellest month. But surely December runs it a close second. The trees seem dead: as Shakespeare called them, 'bare ruined choirs'. On the shortest day we are midway between being worn down by winter and knowing that the days will start to lengthen. It is this gloom and darkness that is a sharp counterpoint to the light we wait for at Christmas. December seems low.

We need to look the darkness and lack of life straight in the eye. This fragment from a poem by Victoria Field is all about loss – the loss of that which sustains us and every living entity. Without the sun, we are nothing.

In this short poem there is something delicious about the weather and the gloom and the birds sense it – live it, even. And there is a hint of peace and hope. We are at the shortest day, the birds know. But the days must get longer, and although a while off, spring will come.

———————

Prayer

Father, perhaps we all understand something of the meaning of loss. Loss often comes when we least expect it and its impact is devastating. When we lose our way of life and the things we love doing, it leaves us confused and sometimes angry. We wonder when things will ever be the same again. Let us remind ourselves that Advent is all about new beginnings and new realities. In this season, we miss the sun and the warmth, and we prepare ourselves for more months of winter but knowing that Advent says that love wins and that hope is the most powerful currency we have.

Amen.

———————

Teaching

Matthew 21:23–27
So they answered Jesus, 'We don't know' (v. 27).

Knowledge sometimes feels like light and ignorance like darkness. The danger in that is that we lose the art of living with mystery and develop instead an addiction for 'certainty', which we mistake for light.

Do you love being certain? Do you like tidy answers that are binary, 'yes or no?' Do you like being informed of those answers, or are you happy working them out for yourself? In the dim perpetual twilight of this mid-Advent period, there are a lot of shades of grey. That sense of uncertainty and that life is conditional is present in the extract from the poem. It is the very opposite of a kind of black-and-white certainty.

Jesus' authority was often challenged, and he was often asked questions. It's amazing to know how infrequently he gave a straight answer. When he asks the priests where John the Baptist's authority had come from, he gives them not an answer, but a question. They see the trap, and decide to reply, 'We don't know.' Interestingly, the question arises immediately after Jesus cleansed the temple. He provoked the angry, defensive reaction precisely because he had rejected the way in which the priests and the temple authorities had reduced God's house to a 'system'.

There is a pattern here. Instead of giving them the answer, Jesus lets them work it out for themselves, and it is in the working out that we really learn from God. Jesus always compelled his listeners to go away and figure things out – he very seldom gave it to them on a plate (John 16:25).

We are invited to look at the grey sky, the bare trees and the rapidly fading sun, and confront its questions. I have found that to be true all through my life. There is no doubt that God has come through and answered prayer. But in all things, I have been required to work things out, to apply myself and to go through the painful exercise of participating with God, not just sitting back and waiting for the divine postman to arrive.

Furthermore, I have received great joy and release by allowing myself, by literally giving myself permission, to say 'I don't know.' I smile when I encounter overwhelming certainty about the mysterious things of God. The lifelong search for evidence, apologetics and proof is always so inadequate. I have lived my life in a Christian tribe renowned for its love of 'certainty'.

For in all pursuits of certainty lies the danger of reducing God to our level, and when we do that, it becomes the very opposite of certain – it results in a house built on sand, human understanding, concepts, theories and logic.

There is not much joy there. Psalm 25: 'To you, O LORD, I lift up my soul. O my God, in you I trust' (NRSVA). That means for me that the good news is the good news, and there is no need for a logical explanation. I do not need to know why Jesus did this or said that, I do not know who is in and who is out, just that God affirmed the human race in coming to be a human being.

This 'I don't know' theology inevitably has a name. It is called apophatic theology, which holds that we do best when we stick to saying what God 'is not', that God's essence is indescribable. It is balanced by cataphatic theology – or *positive theology*. This is the belief in the *Incarnation*. God has revealed himself, after all, in the person of Jesus Christ. Advent becomes revelation and mystery at the same time.

There is no system, just Jesus. That is the Christian joy – heavily disguised at times, I acknowledge.

Questions

- How far does your faith rest on having things explained and logical? Can you allow some space for mystery and uncertainty?
- Can you learn to love the grey shades of Advent, or do you prefer the lighter, brighter times of certainty?
- If something is best accepted as inexplicable or paradoxical, can you accept it as true?

Tuesday 3

Close to Joy

In this present, praise Heaven's Host
Our Maker's might, and moving thought.
His wondrous works that are the wonder of all.
Everlasting Lord and Unmoved Mover
Who fashioned first for earth's kind
A heaven overhead – Hail Holy Creator!
Then this earth – Ah, Mankind's Keeper!
Lord always, who afterwards adorned
This with His earth,
All powerful Presence.

*'Caedmon's Hymn', translated from the Anglo-Saxon,
Patricia and William Oxley*[19]

Caedmon is a beautiful saint – well, aren't they all? This translation of a hymn he wrote points to why he was so inspiring

and filled with holiness. He understood the very nature and essence of joy.

The joy that is tantalisingly close, and which we celebrate at Advent, is the profound culmination of all that is good and true. Our ancestors saw God in everything. For them, of course, the Incarnation (God among us) made perfect sense. God made the earth and all that is in it, so why wouldn't he want to stand in solidarity and love beside his creation? This is his earth and he doesn't just look on from afar.

In the small and fragile infant Christ there is still the all powerful presence of the mighty God of sea and storm.

———————————

Prayer

Father, we join with the sentiment and words of this ancient hymn. We look around us and see that you made everything, and you did so in love and creativity. We thank you that you are close. We know that you love the whole world and everyone and everything in it, so help us not to become too narrow in the way we think about salvation. Join us with the ancients and the saints who have gone before us in the prayer of appreciation for all that you are.

Amen.

———————————

Teaching

Matthew 21:28–32 The Story of Two Sons

'Everlasting Lord and Unmoved Mover', says Caedmon. The language is unfashionable today, and implies a great question within us, the question of obedience. I'm not even comfortable typing the word. One of the questions of Advent is, will you respond to this move of God by choosing to be part of it? And if so, are you willing to be obedient? The Advent model of obedience is Mary, I suppose.

Jesus tells us a story of two sons, requested by their father to tend the family vineyard. One says yes, but doesn't do it. One says no, but thinks better of it and obeys.

We all think that we get joy from getting what we want, and feel unhappy when we have to do things that someone else asks us to do. It is almost as if they are robbing us of our own personal time. It feels like theft, not joy. Time is scarce, and a day I spend serving someone else is a day I won't get back.

The problem is this seldom gives me joy. The focus on self eventually makes me irritable, and there is release when I finally change my mind. I am literally like Jonah running from God and finding myself in a little mental storm of my own making, until I relent, and say 'yes'.

Jesus' story contains not a command but a request. The yes/no decision is not a master–slave response, but a Father–child one. Obedience is not about dutiful forelock tugging because that makes you miserable as well. The second son's decision is selfish, but it convicts him, and he changes his mind, not because his dad is angry, but because he knows he is hurting the one who loves him.

The other son has fallen into a different trap. He thinks it's OK to outwardly look obedient and say the right things. This is also a false joy, based on the fleeting affirmation of looking good. This is more pernicious; my goodness, how much Christian life slips through our fingers because we have sated our consciences by making the right noises or good appearances. But there is no joy in either wilful disobedience or passive disobedience. In neither case do we connect with the heart of God.

In its way, the ancient poem at the start of the day explains why we might be obedient and how we might get joy. Look around, the poet says. God is close. The Father made all this for you. Do not run off and pursue your own selfish agendas. Christian joy is not in obeying the rules because they are rules; it is about connection with a family relationship. God never lets us go, so joy lies in making the connection with the heart of God.

The coming of Jesus affirmed humankind as a co-worker with God the Father. We obey because God is asking us to do the right thing – to work in the vineyard. The grapes do not pick themselves and the eventual outcome will be gorgeous, wholesome wine which will bless the Father, the sons, and all the people. Letting the grapes rot may yield up a bit of free time, but the joy of that is totally ephemeral.

Which of us will obey the Father?

Questions

- Can you find joy in obeying God? Can you discover the life source in it rather than mere duty?
- What is the Father asking you to do? What might the outcome of obedience be? What might the wine taste like?
- What is the outcome of saying no? Might something wonderful be lost?

Wednesday 3

The Doors to Joy Will Open

And doors will open, as in dreams, to flood
Our drab existences with undreamt light
And beckon us into a world as bright
As all the dreams that once flowed in our blood;
And we, custodians of our sacred dust,
Curators of the relics of our past,
Will stare dumbfounded at a hope too vast
To find space in our hearts, unused to trust.
We might, although we rarely do, walk out
Into that other world we thought we'd lost;
We will, more probably, assess the cost
And look for solace in our sense of doubt.
But when we die, I know, we'll see that light;
And God help him who cannot take the sight.

'And Doors Will Open', Jonathan Steffen[20]

I have often wondered about the nature of joy and why it seems so elusive. Sometimes we seem surrounded by it and at others it feels like a long-distant country on the other side of the world.

I once spoke to an elderly Catholic priest and asked him when he most felt a sense of joy. He told me that one day he came into his study, pulled the curtains and the light flooded in. At that moment the room was full of God. He told me that he felt that even the dust particles in the air were dancing for joy.

The poet also is wondering about joy. He is in good company, as a certain John Keats was also doing the same thing many years earlier. Jonathan Steffen ponders the fragility of joy, not because of joy itself, but because we are suspicious of it and find it hard to trust. He wonders if we can ever wrap ourselves in its embrace this side of the grave. Perhaps he wonders if there is a cost to joy, as well.

God understands fragility. After all, he made himself the most fragile thing imaginable – a newborn child. But the poet knows something deep in his soul. One day we will see the full light of God and all the joy that trails along with it.

———————————

Prayer

Father, in all our doubts and weaknesses we still yearn for you. In this season we also think not just about now, but about the end-times. There will be a time when you return in your glory. Let us join with the poet and commit ourselves to that glorious day and the light that we will be bathed in. We know that many things during our life will never be quite as we want them, but as Christmas Day comes into view, we allow ourselves to begin to feel the joy and the wonderment of the God who made the universe being one of us now and forever. Help us not to run from you and to be comfortable knowing that you are close.

Amen.

———————

Teaching

Isaiah 45:6–8,18,21–25
I form the light and create darkness, I bring prosperity and create disaster; I, the LORD, do all these things (v. 7).

I am going to focus on an odd verse, all the odder because this week's theme is 'Joy'. When Jesus came to earth, he experienced human joy in his family and in his friends. But he experienced the full spectrum of human pain as well. The reality of the pain emphasizes the reality of the joy. In a mysterious way, the latter depends on the former.

Isaiah 45:7 says that all things come from God, whether they be bad or good: 'I form the light and create darkness.' This is a challenging statement about the sovereignty and the responsibility of God. The context is the fate of Israel, as God uses the Persian king Cyrus to release them from Babylonian captivity. God is in charge. Both the pain you experience and the joy of release are ultimately down to me, because there is no other God but me, he says.

The life we lead is a rich tapestry full of many coloured strands. It is no life at all if it does not contain some hardship and challenge, and a miserable one if there is no joy. They work together to bring about the reality and the depth of the human condition. Both, in a very real sense, have their final origins in God. The fact that both come from God suggests to me that true joy comes from a comprehension and an empathy with human pain *as well*.

This is hard to accept. There is no philosopher, no intellectual, no genius, and no person of any faith, who can abolish the darkness. It is with us; to some extent, it helps to shape us. The whole point of Christian joy is that the light overcomes it. That is the gospel. There is peace through your pain, before there is an end to pain itself – that essentially is what life is all about. God is present in everything, and redeeming and saving everything, and he leads us through to the other side. The eternal example is Jesus who entered a world of pain, embraced its pain, and ascended to heaven to take everyone with him.

Without that realization, life becomes a litany of disappointment and misunderstanding of the tension between light and darkness, until such a time when there is no darkness at all. That time is not now. The joyful message of Advent is that 'The light shines in the darkness, and the darkness has not overcome it' (John 1:5), a statement read out in almost every carol service.

Advent alerts us to the action of God to enter the darkness, dispel it, and guide us through it by walking alongside us. Understanding what that means is a lifetime's journey of questioning and prayer. It is about helping us to have access to a vast hope, that can be hard to grasp this side of the grave. As the poet told us, we tend to sidestep joy by asking what it will cost us and slipping into doubt.

Questions

- What do you think the darkness actually is? What do you classify as darkness and how does the light of Christ help?
- How has God used challenging situations to shape you? Is hardship always 'darkness', or sometimes just light in disguise?

Thursday 3

The Ghosts of Christmas Past

They gather as the light falters
on a winter's afternoon,
moving silently over the lawn
where rust-coloured leaves collect in clusters.

Drawn by the flicker of candles, they hover
close to windows. I catch the scent
of their presence, the trace of a handprint,
a hint of breath as the glass mists over.

Beneath the antlered branches of elms
they linger in the dusk, their voices
rising uninvited, their faces
reflected in the fire's flames.

Their embers burn within me, their shadows
haunt. Whenever I deck the fir

with tinsel or light the Christmas star,
I sense them looking over my shoulder,

as if I'm a memory, a link to a past
that stretches back down the ages
across long chains of Christmases
to touch a mystery, not yet lost.

'The Christmas Ghosts', Doreen Hinchliffe[21]

Christmas is one of those powerful times that we remember from our childhoods. I grew up in a very secular household – although we did sometimes go to church on Christmas Eve. Although we didn't actively believe, we didn't actively disbelieve. My parents would probably think of themselves as CofE although they didn't go to church.

For the poet, every Christmas is somehow connected to every other Christmas. However secular Christmas has become, we can't quite cut the chains of Christmases over the ages. Amid the presents and the puddings and the lounging in the armchair there is still a mystery at the heart of Christmas. That mystery still hangs over this wintertime celebration.

I do agree, in that there is a mysterious quality to the Incarnation. That God chose to enter the world as one of us needs a big stretch of the imagination to take in. That there might be more to this world than we can touch and feel is also part of the beautiful mystery not just of being, but of celebrating the infant Christ. As we decorate the tree and get the Christmas lights out of the loft or garage, we are taking part in a celebration that stretches into antiquity and with it the wild hope that God is close and always will be.

———————

Prayer

Father, in our modern world it's so easy to race straight to Christmas and to forget about Advent. We don't want to do this, but we allow ourselves today to think about some of the anticipation we're feeling and how Christmas can sometimes be much more complicated than it seems. We all live with the ghosts of other Christmases and we all hope that this one might be different.

As we decorate our trees and get ready for Christmas let us ponder the great story of Christ's life from his conception through to his birth and childhood.

Lord, help us to see how astounding it all is.

Amen.

———————

Teaching

Matthew 1:1–17 The Genealogy of Jesus

'I sense them looking over my shoulder, as if I'm a memory,
a link to a past that stretches back down the ages'

While we are thinking of ghosts, Matthew's gospel begins with a huge list of people who had lived and died long before Jesus came. This list is something that looks irrelevant and very dull. It is a genealogy, and because it's in the lectionary, every now and again this is actually read out in the worship service. And it sounds odd and seems pointless. But actually, that genealogy is a centuries-old memory of promise.

Matthew's purpose is two-fold, and both combine to portray a message of joy through the fulfilment of promise. Advent is a progressive, joyful realization that Jesus was not an out-of-the-blue occurrence, but the long-awaited outcome of an ancient promise and plan. These names are the golden thread of God's intentionality through the centuries.

Firstly, Matthew is stressing the continuity between the Israel of the Old Testament and Jesus. The Old Testament is not 'exorcized', it is fulfilled. Matthew writes primarily to Jewish Christian readers, and grounds all his claims about Jesus in the Old Testament promises of God. Israel's experience of God was real, formative and preparatory, both for the coming of Christ and for the understanding of the world. We see and understand God though the Old Testament.

The second objective is to lay out Jesus' royal lineage as 'son of David'. In 2 Samuel 7:16 God promises David that his kingdom and throne will be established forever. No literal human dynasty could be established forever; we see kingdoms come and go, empires rise and fall. But the reality of the Incarnation, culminating in the Ascension, means that humanity is now fairly established on something that cannot ever be torn down.

This information gives us assurance and validates what we believe. God is seen as faithful and in control. The memory is not a fading ghost, wandering unhappily between worlds, and seen only by cranks and enthusiasts. What we believe in is real, and founded on old, old promises by a God that does not change. The fulfilment of the promise of God makes us safe, even if our journey is eventful. In that we can be joyful.

Questions

- Can you see God's plan unfolding in the past history of your life?
- Can that help you build a more confident faith in the shifting sands of life?

Friday 3

Wonderment

Flying from Heathrow Terminal 5 that day
we threw what food was left for a picnic
into a plastic bag which would have to be empty
before Security. Four hard boiled eggs,
slices of wholemeal bread, a can of Guinness,
one tomato, some walnuts, and found a table
on the top floor Caffè Nero with a view east
toward London towers across runways and grass
over which great winged shadows met their makers
periodically as planes touched down, silently,
to us, through the insulated panoramic glass,
while we peeled our eggs and broke bread.
Miracles repeated become banal, an aeroplane
a minute, like eggs landing on a conveyor belt,
and would we even blink if one skyliner
suddenly began beating its great swan wings,
craning its neck upward uttering bird cries

and took off with its cargo of strapped-in humans
never to be seen again this side of sanity?

'Terminal 5', William Furley[22]

You may be scratching your collective heads and wondering what a poem featuring a can of Guinness and some hard-boiled eggs is doing in a Christian book about Advent. Well, hold that thought.

I have long thought that wonderment is one of those great secrets of the Christian faith. The world is a wonderful place and creation sings out God's glory. And Advent is a time of wonder – a time when we prepare for the appearance of God among us.

We can so easily be blunted to wonder. The poet describes beautifully the wonder that he and his companion have stopped noticing. Amid the snacks and the runway and the terminal, there are magical metal birds flying and we don't even stop to think about it.

As we approach the great time ahead, we need to sharpen our awareness of wonder and be prepared to see things anew. The world is quiet and awaiting a time when the angels will sing and the shepherds will come. But that's just the event itself.

There is something truly wonderful in the merest thought that God might be born in an out of the way place and bring hope to all. We are like those jaded travellers in Terminal 5. I want to experience the wonder all over again. What if the aeroplane suddenly became a giant and beautiful swan flapping its majestic wings and taking people who knows where? What if God stepped from heaven and swooped down into our reality?

––––––––––––

Prayer

Father, renew our sense of wonder in this season. Help us to be like children again, seeing afresh the beauty and joy around us. Help us to take the familiar story of Advent and Christmas and hear it all over again as though we had never heard it before.

Amen.

––––––––––––

Teaching

Jeremiah 23:5–8
The LORD Is Our Righteousness (v. 6, NLT).

'Miracles repeated become banal', says the poet, observing one 747 after another hauling themselves off the tarmac, into the sky. Unlike those who first witnessed the early days of flight, we have lost our wonder.

The same is true of our religious statements. Great poetry slips into a passive banality, losing the wonder of what they say, all the more so if the line ends up in a hymn or a song, that we just mime without thinking.

'The LORD Is Our Righteousness.' What can that mean, and so what?

This is one of the names of God in the Old Testament, 'Yahweh Tsidkenu', or 'The Lord our Righteousness'. A good God is a miracle that we have stopped seeing as a miracle. There are no compelling logical reasons why God should be 'righteousness', no necessity for 'God' to be good, loving or even to care very much about anything. Our reality could be based on a simple conflict between good and evil, with no guarantee as to the victor. The wonderment of the Advent message, and its fulfilment of the promises in the Old Testament, is that God is our righteousness – creation is good, and life is based on an original blessing which never goes away.

The second miracle is that he has made *us* 'good'. We are OK in his sight. Again, it is repeated so often that we lose sight of it.

In the New Testament the apostle John makes a similar dogmatic statement about God: God is love (1 John 4:8). Again, that is not a given – God might not be love. The joy of the Christian message is lost in the tendency for us all to stop wondering about what it might be like if God was not our righteousness, or God was not love. What would life, consciousness and reality be like then?

That is not just a case of what God does. An unjust king can do just things if he is in the mood. This is a statement of what God is – he is the essence of what we call 'righteousness' in his very being, and eternal reality is based on his nature. Reality actually is God-shaped, and it is 'very good' (Gen. 1:10,12,18,21,25,31). Jesus, the Incarnation, assumes it in human form, and affirms it.

The inner joy of that comes from the knowledge that the king came and now reigns. And it continues because we know that our future, and the future for the whole world and creation itself, is founded on righteousness, not the arbitrary rule of the market or the law of the jungle. It is a cause for wonderment.

Our spiritual palettes become blunted; we do not see the wonder at our fingertips. At the centre of life and the universe is God who in his very nature is all good, kind and gracious. The poet realizes that the aircraft taking off from Terminal 5 are a wonder, created by us humans. There is an even greater wonder, though. We were made by God and given the creativity and inspiration to make huge metal flying birds.

Questions

- Do you consider creation fallen or indeed bad? Is it possible that creation is good because God is good?
- Can that in any way change your outlook on life?

Saturday 3

Singing New Songs

Sing to the LORD a new song,
    for he has done marvellous things;
his right hand and his holy arm
    have worked salvation for him.

Psalm 98:1

I have a problem with triumphalism in Christianity. It comes in all shapes and sizes. Perhaps it's because I'm an old misery, but I think that lament and celebration sometimes go side by side. When we sing a new song, we do so because we know that the old song has become dried up or difficult.

The teaching today looks at the escape from barrenness. The joy of being able to conceive is all consuming and, quite rightly, voices are raised to God in thanks. But amid that thanks will always be the memory of what it was like not to have the thing that you most wanted.

The psalmist today urges us to sing a new song to the Lord. I wonder what that new song is? The psalmist reminds us that God has done marvellous things and that he is the God who saves.

If we had just this new song, we would picture the mighty God but not the God that we could really and truly relate to in all our ups and downs. Advent is about the coming of God but also the saving plan of God. He didn't just come to make us feel a bit better. He came as part of the project to save the world and everything in it. We are saved from something and to something. To the living God.

———————

Prayer

Father, I have no problem knowing that you are mighty. But help me to know that when we sing our songs to you, we are singing to the God who is our friend and helper. We all need to sing a new song sometimes as the ones we already have become dried up. In Advent we ask you to renew our faith.

Amen.

———————

Teaching

Judges 13:2–7,24–end

Luke 1:5–25
Your wife Elizabeth will bear you a son (v. 13).

'Sing to the LORD a new song, for he has done marvellous things.' That is what we are saying. His self-revelation in Jesus demonstrates it. It's not religious holy speak – it affects real lives, and it heals genuine, deep-seated pain.

Today we read of two women linked by one affliction: they are 'barren', which means that they are unable to bear children. They feel that they will never get to sing a new song at all. This is a common condition even today and causes genuine misery and disappointment. In the world of the Bible it was tantamount to a curse from God. Whatever else might have been right in life, this cloud of barrenness hung over the woman concerned for her whole life. It was a barrier to joy and often meant a denial of respect and social acceptability. It was not just unfortunate, it was a stain on identity and implicitly always blamed on the woman herself, the very last person who deserved it.

The deliverance from barrenness is only the first level of meaning here. These women had their curse lifted and were given the joy of a child. But their joy is symbolic of something else. They were no longer taboo, no longer outcast, no longer the subject of covert tittering and rejection. They were no longer the subject of pity, the worst kind of human response.

The ending of barrenness meant an end to exclusion. The barren woman image is a representation of all our social constructs of exclusion. God proclaims that none of it is forever and none of it is acceptable. The encounter with God, in Christ who is coming, makes us all 'in' and part of the story.

The healing of Hannah and Elizabeth not only prepares the way for Jesus but is symbolic of the healing of us all. Humanly, we are all barren and fruitless outside of our identity in God. We are excluded from that identity by our guilt and shame, which becomes a vicious circle, creating more guilt and shame. The joy of the Christmas story is that the vicious circle is broken. Behold, I bring tidings of great joy to all people (see Luke 2:10) is the familiar theme.

The Lord has released us from misery into joy by making us fruitful. That is worth singing about, not just because we have benefited, but because it means the world is more beautiful than we could ever have imagined.

Questions

- Are there places in your life which you consider to be barren? Do you long for more fruitfulness in areas of your life?
- Can you see that Jesus' affirmation of the excluded (chronicled all through the gospels, but especially in Luke), is a pattern? That is what God is like.

WEEK 4

Love

Of course you can hang what you wish from me:
I bear the weight of angels very lightly,
And all the coloured kitsch that shines so brightly
From hallowed shopping mall to Christmas tree.
Baubles and lights and tinsel you may load,
And all the hovering ghosts of Christmas past,
And presents, presents, presents – all the vast
Array of what you won't need on the road.
And I shall hold the whole of it for you:
The candles weeping with the joy of birth,
The coolly distant stars that shine on earth
As if their unheard music might ring true.
You can hang many things from me: the bands
To wrap a baby in. Or tortured hands.

'Advent 4', Jonathan Steffen[23]

Whenever life crowds me out or leaves me feeling broken, I think about the Christ and the way he took on trouble and discouragement. Advent is about the holy birth, the battle between good and evil and, of course, the Incarnation. If I were God, I would stay in comfort in my heaven. I would avoid pain and seek pleasure. I might delegate the uncomfortable or dirty tasks to people I could pay, and look away when I realized their servitude and unhappiness. That's what I would do; at least, it is what I would do on my worst day. But I have hope, because of Christ among us, that I might be a better man than that.

When I was badly ill, I went to a clinic in Germany. While there, a doctor took me under his wing and we remained friends, long after my recovery. One day we spoke about faith and I told him that I had become a Christian. He said to me, 'I know, Steven.' He told me that he, too, had become a Christian. He then said this. 'I was always haunted by the Nazi past of my country. I worried that if I were a young man at the time I might have been a guard at a concentration camp and not resisted in any way. That I might have been a monster. It haunted my waking hours. But now that I have God beside me, I know that I would not do it.'

The poet pictures the blessed Christ as a Christmas tree. With the baubles and fun of Christmas hung on him. But the pregnancy of Mary and the birth of her child set the scene for the final battle between good and evil, and in that battle it is God himself who takes the pain and ridicule upon himself.

Sunday 4

If We Met an Angel

How did the angel come? The air grew cold,
Cold with the knowledge of foreknowledge, chilled
With the recognition of a truth unwilled,
Unsought, foretold, and yet not real, not told.

How did the angel look? The small room span,
Span through the ring of birth and death, and swirled
Through the past and future of an alien world
That ached to understand the Son of Man.

How did the angel speak? Without a voice,
And coming from some place within her heart
That seemed not to be hers, discrete, apart,
Entirely other. And she had no choice.

'The Annunciation', Jonathan Steffen[24]

The Annunciation is full of mystery. Painters and artists have taken it to themselves – fascinated by the story of the meeting of a teenage girl with the Angel of the Lord.

In my ministry as a parish priest, I have met many people who have told me about encounters with angels. I don't doubt them, these stories usually have the ring of truth. People report a strange normality about it, but also that feeling of being in a new place of otherness. Whatever the case, we never forget our angelic encounters. And angels seem to know how confronting their presence is because they always begin by asking us not to be in fear.

The poet wonders what Mary would have felt and seen. Perhaps the angel would have been cramped in a small room. What do angels speak like? The poet wonders if they speak direct to the heart but always have that sense of otherness – oddness, even.

The poet thinks that Mary had no option other than to go ahead with what was suggested. On this, I beg to differ. I think she just wanted to know what might be ahead of her and then took the risk, come what may.

––––––––––––

Prayer

Father, we are inspired by the story of Christ's mother. Help us to see in the angel's meeting with her the possibility of us also being very close to them as well. Help us to learn from her good sense and faithfulness. Let us rejoice in Christ's earthly mother as we think about his birth. Help us to honour our own mothers who went through the same pain of childbirth as Mary.

Amen.

Teaching

Luke 1:26–38 The Annunciation

I remember very few dreams. I can recall some, and they have been disturbing, leaving me shaken and almost grateful to be awake. Not nightmares exactly, just confrontations with scenes that were not real.

When we have a true encounter with God, it will conflict with our conditioning. God will speak in many ways, including in dreams, in spirit, in teaching, or through our emotions. If that encounter is really God, that conditioning, that which we have been trained to believe in, takes a backseat. Our training becomes merely groundwork – it enables us to process what we see, but it cannot explain it.

So, when the encounter happens we can either reject it and dig our heels in because it contradicts our theology, or we can let the theories go for a minute, thanking the past for its help, and then allow God to take us up to climb to something higher.

Mary could not possibly have been intellectually prepared for Gabriel's message. There was nothing in the temple, the synagogue, or first-century Judaism to help her with this one. For her to say 'let it be as you say', she had to be prepared to set it aside and go with God. To where? Well, beyond her religion, way beyond her comfort zone, away from her life plans and ambitions such as they were, and away from the approval of people. That ship at least was about to sail – her conservative, judgemental society would not affirm her.

The story invites us to emulate Mary's attitude. It is a faith journey based on simplicity and trust, in her case with only Joseph to reassure her that it was true. That is a very lonely position, apart from anything else. That is a kind of inner assurance derived from experiencing God – it can feel like rebellion and it can lead to arrogance.

But Mary was not arrogant, she was humble, and that inner authority, when received humbly, will take you way beyond the rules of theology and observance to a sky-high experience of God. There's not much of a safety net up there; that's why we revere people like Mary.

Questions

- We often ask God to speak to us. Do we really mean it?
- What do we expect God to say? Will he affirm all our current decisions, or will he challenge them?

Monday 4

The Meaning of Love

Shall we not be sad to die
And hear no more the sounding sigh
Of moorland wind or mottled sea,
Or see still mornings red with light
Above the suburbs where you and me
Kissed each other late at night?

Should we not be happy to have known
In this world it's not unknown
To share a love that joins us to
All things that are, or may occur?
Say yes, dear one, that this is true:
Love is the sole undying spur,

The breath that never breathes its last.
Watch life's clouds pile high and fast,
Leaves curl up and soon decay

And the best eyes lose at length their sight,
But love, like hope, won't go away
For it, like us, belongs to light.

'The Ownership of Light', William Oxley[25]

We continue our journey towards light – 'the true light', as St John calls it. That light is, and has always been, love. As we think about the Light of the World coming into the world, we also think about our own mortality. Looked at in perspective, what does our life add up to?

The love of the God who came into the world is mirrored in each loving relationship we have. As the poet says – love is the sole undying spur. It is our legacy and is eternal. It is the breath that never ceases. While everything else around us perishes and decays, it is love that will not go away.

That is, of course, at the heart of the Incarnation. Jesus didn't come to us as a message or way of proving a point. He came because he loves this world and he could do nothing else. That is why he is the light above all lights and that is why we are people of profound hope. As William Oxley helps us to understand – we belong to light and this season is the one where we celebrate the light breaking through into all that is dark.

———————

Prayer

Father, thank you that light and hope will not go away. In this dark time of the year, lighten our hearts, lift our souls and help us prepare to rejoice with the angels.

Amen.

———————————

Teaching

Zephaniah 3:14–18
The LORD your God is with you, the Mighty Warrior who saves. He will take great delight in you; in his love he will no longer rebuke you, but will rejoice over you with singing (v. 17).

I am a terrible singer unless the song is in exactly the right key and doesn't have too many different notes. Vocal range is something that happens to other people. I also like listening and thinking to sung worship, so rejoicing with singing is a foreign picture to me, it is not how I do it. I'm more likely to sort of raise an eyebrow or give a thumbs-up, or maybe clap. I possess a vast amount of recorded music, but you would not come to my record collection for a party playlist, trust me.

So, when it comes to rejoicing over anything with singing, I can take it or leave it. Moreover, when it comes to God rejoicing and singing over me, I am completely dumbfounded.

That is something I cannot imagine. The only person who has ever sung over me was a musician in a Spanish restaurant. It didn't feel good. I don't think it ended well.

That's because I, like many people, find it hard to love myself. I am mindful of the fact that we have a rightful duty to worship God. The unfortunate undertone is that we come from a place of worthlessness and effectively beg for his forgiveness. The phrase from the Eucharistic prayer about not being worthy to gather the crumbs from under his table comes to mind. I say it because I'm the vicar, but I don't identify with it. I really think it is an unhelpful statement.

Far be it from me to suggest that we are not in need of God's forgiveness or that we don't fall short of God's glory (Rom. 3:23). The entire story of salvation is based on the realization that we cannot save ourselves, and that there is something to be saved from.

But God's story, the narrative of the Old and New Testaments, has a constant theme that must be there for any of it to make sense. God rejoices over his creation from Genesis 1 to Revelation 22, and humanity is the pinnacle of that creation. It is also the focus of his attention.

The fact is that the so-called angry God of the Old Testament often talks about his people like that. Although Israel's behaviour grieves him, God is in love with his people, and they are his pride and joy. Far from the vengeful, self-obsessed God of judgement, God is god of 'covenant', or irrevocable promise where he does the blessing for the sake of his people. If he is bothered about himself, it's only for the sake of his name, reputation and character.

The God of love is more than the God who is sometimes inclined towards love. He does not change. God rejoices over you and me with singing because love always has an object – it is an outward-bound emotion. If it can justifiably be self-directed, then that lies in the mystery of the Trinity and I leave that to others, and another day.

'He will rejoice over you with singing': if we could really understand why God says that, it would transform our image of ourselves and unleash such joy that the world would change. We can travel a very great distance indeed towards healthy self-worth and self-love, towards seeing us as God sees us, without stepping into the trap of pride and self-sufficiency.

God rejoices over us with singing. No matter what your shortcomings may be, if you could believe about yourself what God believes about you, it would change your life. You would be unstoppable. As the poet realized, love won't go away. Why? Because there is a divine source to it.

Questions

- Can you imagine God rejoicing over you with singing?
- If you can imagine *yourself* loving and rejoicing over an imperfect person, why is it so hard that God would rejoice over you?

Tuesday 4

The Cost of Love

Six of us perhaps had already passed
and it was you, my friend, with whom I walked,
who noticed first the baby rabbit
bang in the middle of the lane, on its side,
an eye open, lightly breathing, barely living.

Clearly we had to put it from its misery.
I remembered killing a broken-winged pigeon
with a shovel, how it took two whacks at least,
how something inside it refused to die
or something inside me lacked courage to kill.

But you looked about, saw a single old glove,
mangy, filthy, forgotten at the wayside,
and declared *that's what it's there for*,
took it from its yellowed plot, curled it in your palm,
and tenderly scooped up the baby rabbit,

and set it upright off the beaten track. We stared
for half a minute: no motion, but no death either.
You were sanguine: better closer to the earth,
come life or death, than exposed on the path.
I was waiting for you, so you moved first.

I was waiting because whatever sentimental
anthropomorphism I had just witnessed
seemed not that at all, but a lesson in love,
and you do not leave before your teacher.
And you may wish one day for such a glove.

'The Glove', Wynn Wheldon[26]

My word, I have needed just this kind of gloved compassion
at times in my life. I have sometimes thought that it might
be best to put me down and get on with it. But each time,
someone has not given up on me.

Advent is the clear truth that God does not and will never
give up on us. But we need people to teach us how to love.
The poet knows this and so does each of us. Love is catching –
it is the ultimate reason to keep breathing.

Christ is born from love and into love. He is surrounded by
family and the heavenly hosts. His birth argues against bru-
tality and says that he is the source of the kind of love that
doesn't put an animal out of its misery but gives it the gentle
help to have another chance.

The poet shows that we always have choices and that one of
those choices is to be the gentle glove around the despair and

hopelessness of another. On the face of it the two options in this poem are both loving. There is the option to put the animal out of its misery. Is that love? To spare the creature from future pain. Any vet is faced with this dilemma every day. There is another option in this case. To gently move the creature to a safer place and to do so knowing that it may still die. Why not gently put us in a far safer place?

Safety is something that most of us yearn for. Life is contingent and difficult. God could have decided it was too risky to come among us as a defenceless child. But he didn't.

———————————

Prayer

Father, thank you for this beautiful picture of compassion and gentleness. Let us know that you are the author of all compassion and gentleness as well. We pray for all those who are in need of care and love in this season. We know that many people become sad in the run-up to Christmas. They are lonely and it is a time when we remember the people we love who are no longer with us. Surround us with friends who can cheer us up and take us out of ourselves.

Amen.

———————————

Teaching

Luke 1:46–56 The Song of Mary – The Magnificat

God loves us so much that sometimes he takes away the things we love too much.

I enjoy the things I have. I am so lucky that each Christmas now I have problems telling my nearest and dearest what to get me for Christmas. I am possession-laden; my daily routine is almost controlled by when, how and where to re-charge the things I have. Phones, laptop, tablet, digital radio, Bluetooth devices, camera batteries – you name it, I possess it, and I must recharge it. I am overrun with 'stuff'. I have no interest in clothes but still cannot move for them. I have so many books I have run out of shelves, even in a purpose-built study in a vicarage.

As I meditate on this, I am sheepishly aware that these things constitute a form of distraction. They are a form of mighty power over me, that must be torn down. Maintenance, fear of loss, and the need for novelty (more stuff!) is an addic-tion. Things are not a good medium for God at all, they are a barrier. The kingdom of God is a place in each person's heart where God 'reigns', and anything that prevents that happen-ing is a problem. This is not a trivial thing, my entire entou-rage is both idol, and co-dependency; I depend on it, and it depends on me if only to be recharged!

Mary sings of the things that block the kingdom: the proud, the mighty and the rich – power, prestige, and stuff. Her message is that God, passionate about the true welfare of his people, pulls these things down because they are harmful.

It's easy to see the target of these words being people richer than me. This is not just God wreaking vengeance on idolaters, it's the Father weaning his children off their addiction and restoring them to health. Even in our Covid-19 crisis, we have had to re-evaluate what is necessary, helpful and worthy of our time and money. This is usually painful, but we can see it is God's agenda. Many businesses have no doubt failed this year because they no longer passed that test. I wonder if unjust structures, powers and principalities will do the same; that is another matter, I fear.

Advent is about preparing our hearts for love. Love is sometimes hard to accept, and the real reason is that we are ashamed of our fleshly feelings so much that we seek comfort in other things – power, prestige and possessions. Love says, you are OK and you do not need to get comfort from things that do not last or give you joy.

As the gospels play out, we see Jesus will teach remorselessly about the danger of these things and how corrosive they are to the gentle, voluntary, participatory kingdom of God. Jesus will constantly warn us of the cancers of power, prestige and possessions, far more than he ever says about the sort of sin that we focus on. We remain far more inclined to focus on the sins of the flesh than on the wholesale rebellion in our hearts, minds, and spirit away from simplicity and reliance on God, and towards things we own, cherish, and can control.

God the Father loves his children in an unfathomable way, enough to want to wean them off their unhelpful addictions. Putting it that way, it's not so hard to understand.

When we are in the centre of addiction, we feel that we are only heading in one direction. It feels like death. The poet, using the image of the wounded rabbit, shows that love never gives up.

Questions

- What do you need to let go of? Do power, prestige and stuff play too dominant a role in your life?
- Can we accept a God who comes to tear these things down? Or do we want him to do that only to others?

Wednesday 4

Love Defeats Shame

No one who hopes in you
will ever be put to shame . . .

Psalm 25:3

It was my first week at University. I was very nervous, and I seemed to lack the polish of the other students in my seminar group. I suppose I was very aware that I seemed to be the only person who had made it onto the prestigious course from a comprehensive school. During the seminar I managed to mispronounce the name of a rather famous author. I knew I'd done it the minute I said it but the silence that followed was ominous. But what came after was even worse. Our teacher laughed and pronounced the name correctly in a sarcastic voice. When he laughed everyone else laughed. I found myself burning red with shame. I knew that I hadn't had the advantages of those around me and the minute the class began to find my mistake funny, I was totally and completely ashamed.

These days I'm not so easily shamed. I know where I came from and I know I came from very humble beginnings. I have no desire to escape my past, in fact I'm very grateful for it. I make no apology that I wasn't able to go to a more elevated school and that I come from working class roots. The experience of shame is still with me. Of course, love overcomes shame.

Jesus could have come to us as the fully fledged King. He could have been born in a palace and come with the most perfect back story. Instead, he came not just from humble beginnings, but from shameful ones. What does this say about divine love? The people around Mary and Joseph could do maths. They could work out when the boy was born, that the number of months didn't quite add up, and that Jesus had been conceived out of wedlock. In small communities there are long memories, and this stigma would have been with Jesus throughout his childhood and adult life. Christ was born poor, and Christ was born in circumstances that were less than perfect. I think that Christ is looking to rehabilitate us from the shackles of shame. He does this through his perfect love and through his very humble beginnings. He chose to identify with those who are shamed and to show that they are loveable and worthy of the ultimate sacrifice. Shame creeps up on us, but love is stronger still.

———————————

Prayer

Father, thank you so much for liberating us through your love from the prison of shame. Help us not to judge others and to make them feel ashamed. Let us see that our backgrounds are no barrier to your love of us. You came to be with us in circumstances that confounded the rules of propriety and status. Let us live lives of freedom where we help others to move beyond shame and towards love.

Amen.

————————

Teaching

Isaiah 7:14
She will give birth to a son and will call him Immanuel (which means 'God is with us') (NLT).

Here we have the biblical origins of the well-known term for Jesus, Immanuel, God with us. In the Christmas event, in the Incarnation, we can see the heart of God, and the reality of having God with us. What does it show us?

Fundamentally, I believe, it is this: God came to be with us because he wanted to affirm us. It is in the nature of theology to emphasize the fact that he came to 'save us', and this is also true. But that is not the same as saying that he regarded us as shameful, unworthy, and wicked, for that makes no sense.

The incarnation, God with us, is a response of affirmative love, it is not a shaming act. Richard Rohr explains that Jesus did not come to earth to change God's mind about us, he came to change our minds about God.[27]

When we look at Jesus, we do not see the judgemental, vengeful heart of God coming to pronounce judgement upon us and frighten us into humble submission. All of those things would be perfectly justifiable for perfect, holy almighty God to do, but he does not. What he does is to lift those who have been shamed into elevated positions of honour – those guilty of sexual sin, those who extorted taxes from their country-men, those who were Gentile outsiders, women, children, lepers and the unclean . . . the list is endless.

God with us is a fulfilment of all the Scriptures, especially those places that stress that we shall be saved, and our shame be put aside. This is not a matter of just deserts, it is a matter of mercy, but mercy stems from the nature of God and his pure eternal love. He created us for a reason: to show that love.

Questions

- What is your view of why God came to be with us?
- Can you speak to God, or look him in the face, so to speak, and feel affirmed and loved?

Thursday 4

The Poor Will Be Raised from the Dust

The Lord is exalted over all the nations,
his glory above the heavens.
Who is like the Lord our God,
the One who sits enthroned on high,
who stoops down to look
on the heavens and the earth?

He raises the poor from the dust
and lifts the needy from the ash heap;
he seats them with princes,
with the princes of his people.
He settles the childless woman in her home
as a happy mother of children.

Psalm 113:4–9

One of the reasons I'm so attracted to Advent is that it reveals God on a human scale. I wrestle with some of the pictures of God in his glory. It isn't that I don't believe it, it's just that I always feel that a God who is that powerful and high seems way beyond us.

The psalmist begins by painting an extraordinary picture of God in the highest. We see God exalted over all the nations full of glory. He is magnificent and seated on the throne of power. The good news is that he alone can use that power for the good and that he is the source of all justice and love. Advent helps us to see the outworking of God's love and to appreciate where that love is focused.

If God was simply mighty, he might have a hard job winning us to him. Might induces fear and obedience, but rarely love. The psalmist shows the beautiful and subversive way that the God who made the universe really loves us. Advent declares that God is both for us and for those who are of humble origin and who are in trouble. The Christ born in an unglamorous location amongst the domestic animals speaks loudly of the way that God's love seeks to lift the poor and needy and bring them into the centre of all things.

It is easy to say we love someone. But love comes at a cost and it is an action as well as an emotion. Christ, born among the common people and determined to heal the broken-hearted and set the captives free, shows that the God of might is the God of compassion and love and fairness. For this I am very thankful.

Prayer

Father, thank you for the inspiring picture of your greatness and majesty. Help us to take comfort in this and know that everything about you is pointed in the direction of love and compassion. Help us to be instruments of change. This Advent, help us to really know that your might and majesty is on a human scale and that we can approach you without fear.

Amen.

_____

Teaching

Luke 1:39–45
Blessed is she who has believed that the Lord would fulfil his promises to her!

Elizabeth is one of those who exemplifies Psalm 113:9. At the time of her conceiving John the Baptist she was at the point of giving up, and for her the shame of childlessness loomed.

When she encounters Mary, there is an extraordinary thing. Her baby, who will be John the Baptist, leaps for joy in her womb, and she is filled with the Holy Spirit. Why? Because she says, 'There will be a fulfilment'.

The deliverance from barrenness is a fulfilment of promise, it is an act of God who has now done what he said he would do. Furthermore, under the guidance of the Holy Spirit, Elizabeth senses that Mary embodies another fulfilment. In that moment of recognition, she sees the full, awesome faithfulness of God, and his love for all mankind.

God's aim is to raise the unacceptable from their position of exclusion. Both Mary and Elizabeth knew this, even the unborn John realized it. What Elizabeth sees in the face of the pregnant Mary is the salvation plan of God – the restoration of all those considered taboo, be they barren, contagious, disabled or rejected. Those deemed unacceptable are now elevated to the highest height.

Elizabeth and her unborn baby recognize the fulfilment of God's promise to be there for the unacceptable people, those who don't 'measure up'. What we have to ask is how much we follow God's lead? Have we replaced the lepers, the tax collectors and sinners with new categories of our own and even congratulated ourselves for how holy we are? It is a sobering thing to consider God's anger, but even more sobering I find, to confront the challenge of his grace. God loves more people than we want him to.

Questions

- Can you, in Jesus, find comfort for the sense of exclusion or unworthiness you feel?
- Have you created your own 'untouchables'?

Friday 4

Keep Us from Harm

The LORD will keep you from all harm –
he will watch over your life;
the LORD will watch over your coming and going
both now and for evermore.

Psalm 121:7–8

I love the odd paradox of Advent. The God who is our protector also needed protecting. For the God who made the heavens to present himself to us as a helpless baby in a volatile political situation is astounding. That God made himself weak and vulnerable seems to me to be at the heart of love. Love is about risk. When we love, we risk being hurt and we risk making ourselves vulnerable. If we get hurt too often or too deeply then the temptation is to shut up shop and go into our shell. God has taken this risk and continues to do so.

Advent shows us a God who will risk everything for love. The psalmist draws a beautiful picture of the God who will protect us and watch over our lives. I know that I frequently feel a sense of peril and long for protection. This ancient poem reassures me that God isn't just going to protect me from the odd incident, but he is watching me and watching over me for my whole life, and that is quite a commitment. God's love is eternal.

At our memory café, I was always very moved when I saw couples coming whose love refused to die. Even when one of them was suffering from dementia and could no longer recognize their partner, that love was still there in the sacrifices made. To keep loving someone in such demoralizing circumstances is nothing short of a miracle. I find this a source of wonder and comfort.

Love involves sacrifice and God's offer to care for us was embodied in a backwater village on a night when everyone, except a few shepherds, seemed to be asleep. The offer of love is non-conditional and forever. Advent tells us that God stepped into history and put himself at risk. But love, of course, always involves risk.

Prayer

Father, please watch over us and protect us. Let your love cover every part of our lives and be with us in our coming and our going. Help us to offer protection and love to those around us. Help us to spread the good news that love wins.

Amen.

Teaching

> *Luke 2:8–13*
> But the angel said to them, 'Do not be afraid. I bring you good news that will cause great joy for all the people' (v. 10).

God is not as we characterize him; he is not our invention. He does not conform to any of our ideas as to what God should do. The good news relates to the fact that God has come to demonstrate that his protecting hand is over us, not his threatening fist.

The news is first proclaimed to the shepherds. There is nothing particularly necessary that it should be them. It might just as well have been fishermen, or farmers, or carpenters or anyone else.

But the shepherds were symbolic of something. A shepherd was a contradiction: he was the poorest of the poor in paid employment terms, yet a metaphor for care and responsibility. When the nation was in despair and exile, God spoke through Ezekiel to blame the 'bad shepherds' (Ezekiel 34:1–10), namely the nations leaders. The shepherd metaphor actually stood for 'those that exercise a duty of care, safety, and pastoral love'.

In contrast, God is the good shepherd (Ezekiel 34:11–16), searching, rescuing, gathering, feeding, and leading them. The good news was the announcement that the Great Shepherd (Psalm 23) was fulfilling the promises in Psalm 121 to keep us from great harm, to watch over our lives, and to replace the great pagan beliefs in the sun and moon (Psalm 121:6).

The good news is that the Great Shepherd has come to elevate the downtrodden and offer himself as our guardian by choice. He does not impose himself, nor does he operate through the great powers and authorities of the world. Their power is an illusion. He announces himself to the shepherds of the world for he is their true shepherd.

It remains both good news and deep mystery, for the world is still enslaved by injustice and insecurity. So, the call of Advent is to make the leap of faith that, despite appearances, the good news is coming true and will continue to reveal itself as mankind travels nearer and deeper to its true potential in God.

Questions

- How often do you pray for the 'shepherds' of our society, those who are there to lead, steer and protect?
- Who might you seek to elevate today? Do you know any of life's shepherds, someone who does a vital job but isn't appreciated?

Christmas Eve

Nearly There

Midnight. A tabby slinks across the backs,
his fur smoothed by the wind. He slakes his thirst,
moves on. Now's the time insomniacs
like me sip tea, stargaze, wait for the first
grey streak of dawn to light the cobalt sky.
Upstairs, my child fights sleep, hoping to see
a host of eager reindeer flying high
above the roofs. I stand beside the tree,
step over piles of presents stretching far
beyond its branches. Reaching up, I prick
my finger on its pines, wish on its star,
long for a sudden snowfall inches thick
and sense a mystery turning in the air,
like tiny threads of gossamer, angel hair.

'Christmas Eve', Doreen Hinchliffe[28]

Most people are asleep, deep in dreams. But the poet cannot sleep. She is on her own, sipping tea and thinking about her child upstairs and snoozing. I can so understand this, as a parent myself. We so want our children to have 'a magical Christmas' – something that reassures them that a certain gift is at the centre of the world.

The poet is immersed in such thoughts. She looks at the stars and wonders about the morning. Her child dreams of reindeer flying above the rooftops – alive with the magic and mystery of Christmas. But even adults can get an intimation of what it is really all about. Amid the presents and the tinsel, we wonder about that day when God drew truly close – and refuted the accusation of Job that he had no idea what it was really like to be a human person.

Amid the presents, the poet senses a mystery punctuating the air and sprinkling wonderment. She catches the rumour of angels. Those angels are preparing to sing their hearts out.

––––––––––––––––

Prayer

Father, on this still and holy night let us sleep well; the sleep of angels. Help us to appreciate what we have. Let us bless those around us. Let our Christmas Day be good. Help it to be a day of peace and joy and one in which memories are made.

Amen.

––––––––––––––––

Teaching

Luke 1:67–79
. . . because of the tender mercy of our God, by which the rising sun will come to us from heaven to shine on those living in darkness and in the shadow of death, to guide our feet into the path of peace (vv. 78–79).

The breaking of dawn is a most wonderful thing if you are up to see it. It is God's free gift and most of us miss it every day. It is usually accompanied by nature's most generous gift, the dawn chorus of the birds. Even in urban London where I live, the dawn is a beautiful thing, and the chorus is awe inspiring, as each creature sings out its territorial claim to this or that part of my garden. It is so loud where I live that I wonder it never actually wakes me up.

As we sit on the cusp of Incarnation, the dawn is about to break. Like the rising sun it is unstoppable. Like the rising sun its irresistible goal is to bring light to those who have just endured darkness. Jesus came like the dawn, accompanied by a deafening chorus (Luke 2:14).

Because this literally happened 2,000 years ago, we are re-thinking it in metaphorical terms now. This can degenerate into a change of poetic language, and in the face of a global reality that looks challenging, and un-redeemed, it can sometimes just be religious wishful thinking. However, if we dig deeper, we can let its real message out into the light.

The universe and eternity are essentially good, and there is no escape from the light. No one can prevent the dawn, for to do so you must stop the earth from turning or put out the sun. That's how irresistible is the tender mercy of God. Love will win whether you like it or not – just as Hemingway writes, 'the sun also rises' – even if things might be bad right now, dawn is inevitable. God announces hope and joy for the future and wants us to see past and present as part of a greater cycle, leading to an outcome so much larger than anything we have ever known.

That becomes reality if we allow it to. Peace on earth and goodwill to men is God saying, 'I love you: love yourselves and love each other and transform your world with me into what it ought to look like.' This message is not God threatening to wave a stick or a magic wand, but to recreate new people by renewing their hearts. Incarnation people behave differently, and the world changes.

Final Word

Why Advent Matters

Barry Hingston, Harrow, June 2020

I have to say focusing on Advent is a relatively new game for me. I'm a Johnny-come-lately to Anglicanism and church calendars and Advent in my formative years meant a calendar or a candle. It was simply the build-up to Christmas, an opportunity to ask for things and to buy things, and a season of parties of varying degrees of indulgence.

To some extent, Advent has been spoiled or even abolished, transfigured into an elongated season of festivity. The invitation to the party goes out in October and it is in full swing as soon as Remembrance is out of the way. Christmas itself is squeezed into Midnight Mass, and from that point it becomes Yule or some other version of the Roman 'Saturnalia'. If you are going to have an Advent, you are going to have to work at it.

This is a shame because the subconscious lifelong benefit for me has been learning the value of 'delayed gratification'; what you wait for, you value. The word 'Advent' comes from the Latin 'adventus' which means 'coming'. The season is built on the value of anticipation and inner preparation. God does his most interesting work for us when we are waiting for him to act, for it is then that we need to grow in faith and examine ourselves to see how we need to change. Character change takes place in times of waiting – we either choose to wait or we make easier, worse choices. Jesus was 700 years in the waiting from Isaiah's great prophecies, the Holy Spirit was given 800 years after Joel's great prediction, and his next coming is still awaited.

We live in the now-and-not-yet world and it changes us. Remember also that the season also celebrates Jesus' anticipated coming again. We are now in the waiting season for that. Advent time is our whole life's work. Advent reminds us that the question is not whether Jesus will return to judge the earth, but when. Many of the great prophecies in Isaiah and elsewhere have their full significance not just in the first coming, but in the second, or the time between the two.

Before the seventh century, Christmas was a secondary feast but it grew in importance and so Advent did too. The season of Advent came into being in the middle of the sixth century and was established as four Sundays in length by Pope St Gregory the Great (590–604). It became more solemn and its orientation changed from just being a time to prepare for Christmas, to looking to the glorious return of the Lord. The Sundays of Advent reflect this double aspect of waiting for the Second Coming (First and Second Sundays) and preparation for the feast of Christmas (Third and Fourth Sundays).

What we see now has been transformed by the Victorians, the Industrial Revolution, and the Retail Revolution into a simple excuse to stop thinking about the cold. It is a mixture of cosy images, of various forms of lighting, decoration and music. Actually, I like all these things, it's just that Advent is also something else – the transformative impact of waiting.

In that waiting we consider the sweeping narrative of Scripture. We consider the significance of the Incarnation event, and the change in humankind that comes from realizing that God affirms us. We look to the glorious prospect of the kingdom of God, imperfectly inaugurated now, but 'coming'. We consider the reality of darkness and light, especially in the northern hemisphere, and give some space to what that tension means. We look at our own lives and ask ourselves questions.

But we must do that for ourselves. Society will not lay on an 'Advent' for us and has hijacked Christmas many years ago. This engagement with God, and with the spiritual change that can come inside, is a Christmas gift but it is also a 'work'. We need to be intentional about Advent, wait for Christmas and then crank up the joy.

We get the opportunity every year, and each year we promise to do it better next year, just like Holy Week. But no matter, it is still an opportunity. Each year we can concentrate on a new aspect of it, and enjoy the richness, the beauty and the fathomless mystery of Immanuel, God with us. Each year we start again.

How easy to forget we were here before
on a hilltop bared to the sky
where ancient forest is reduced to three –
cherry, hazel and mulberry.

Just enough joy to greet winter's end
just enough wisdom to hold in one hand
sufficient crop to sustain a faith
that we can begin again.

'Hilltop', Tessa Lang[29]

The spires lean
into the air
touch the blue inside
of the sky
lightly
a philosophy
a cathedral
about to lift the world
off its knees

'Chartres Cathedral', Katherine Gallagher[30]

Index of Poems

Notes

[1] 'Robin's Song' published here for the first time.

[2] 'York Minster' previously published in Jonathan Steffen, *St. Francis in the Slaughter-House and Other Poems*, Falcon Editions, 2006 (Audio book).

[3] 'Christmas Haiku 2017' published here for the first time.

[4] 'First Coming' to be published in Anne Pilling, *Ways of Speech*, Shoestring Press, October 2020.

[5] 'Advent 1' published here for the first time.

[6] 'Cemetery Angel' previously published in Jonathan Steffen, *St. Francis in the Slaughter-House and Other Poems*, Falcon Editions, 2006 (Audio book).

[7] 'Evening Prayer' published here for the first time.

[8] 'By Heart' previously published in Alwyn Marriage, *Touching Earth*, Oversteps Books, 2007 and in *Cracking On: Poems on Ageing by Older Women*, Grey Hen Press, 2009.

[9] 'Hope at Year's Turning' previously published in Alwyn Marriage, *Festo: Celebrating Winter and Christmas*, Oversteps Books, 2012.

[10] 'What Are We Waiting For?' previously published in *London Grip New Poetry*, December 2015.

[11] 'Advent 2' published here for the first time.

[12] 'Sleepers' published here for the first time.

[13] 'School of Giotto' published here for the first time.

[14] 'Winter Landscape' previously published in Jonathan Steffen, *The Colour of Love*, Acumen Publications, 2011.

[15] 'Spadework' originally published in Jennie Osborne, *How to be Naked*, Oversteps Books, 2010.

[16] 'Studio' previously published in Jonathan Steffen, *The Colour of Love*, Acumen Publications, 2011. Reprinted in *Poetic Pilgrimages, James Hogg at Eighty*, Poetry Salzburg, 2011.

[17] 'Advent 3' published here for the first time.

[18] 'December' by Victoria Field first appeared in *Many Waters: Poems from Ten Months at Cornwall's Cathedral*, published by Fal Publications, 2006. Used by permission.

[19] This translation of 'Caedmon's Hymn' published here for the first time; original text in Henry Sweet, *An Anglo-Saxon Reader in Prose and Verse*, first published in 1876.

[20] 'And Doors Will Open' previously published in *Acumen Magazine*, Summer 1991.

[21] 'The Christmas Ghosts' previously published in Doreen Hinchliffe, *Substantial Ghosts*, Oversteps Books, 2020.

[22] 'Terminal 5' by William Furley published here for the first time.

[23] 'Advent 4' by Jonathan Steffen published here for the first time.

[24] 'The Annunciation' previously published in Jonathan Steffen, *St. Francis in the Slaughter-House and Other Poems*, Falcon Editions, 2006 (Audio book).

[25] 'The Ownership of Light' published here for the first time.

[26] 'The Glove' first published in Wynn Wheldon, *Tiny Disturbances*, Acumen, 2012.

[27] Richard Rohr, 'Love, Not Atonement', Centre for Action and Contemplation (Thursday, May 4, 2017) https://cac.org/love-not-atonement-2017-05-04/ (accessed 17.09.20).

[28] 'Christmas Eve' previously published in *New Poems for Christmas*, Live Canon Publishing, 2015.

[29] 'Hilltop' by Tessa Lang, 2016, previously unpublished.

[30] 'Chartres Cathedral' © Katherine Gallagher, 1985 from *Passengers to the City* (Hale and Iremonger, 1985) and *Carnival Edge: New and Selected Poems* (Arc Publications, 2010).

9 781788 931960